The Fifties
Replayed

The Fifties Replayed

A Norfolk Youth at Leisure

COLIN MILLER

First published in the United Kingdom in 2008 by
Sutton Publishing, an imprint of NPI Media Group Limited
Cirencester Road · Chalford · Stroud · Gloucestershire · GL6 8PE

British Library Cataloguing in Publication Data
A catalogue record for this book is available from the British Library.

ISBN 978-0-7509-4949-1

I dedicate this volume to the memory of my parents,
Raymond and Gertrude Miller, my grandparents, Walter and Nora Miller
and Arthur and Edith Cole, and to my many uncles, aunts and cousins
who played an important part in my early life.

Typeset in 10.5/13pt Galliard.
Typesetting and origination by
NPI Media Group Limited.
Printed and bound in England.

Contents

Acknowledgements

Writing this book has given me immense pleasure but it would not have been possible without the encouragement and help that I received from many individuals and organisations. I wish to thank my dear wife, Dr Celia Miller, for her patience, encouragement and practical assistance, and my many cousins for sharing their personal experiences with me. I am most grateful for the help given during my research by the staff of the Great Yarmouth Central Library, the Norfolk and Norwich Millennium Library, Archant Norfolk and the University of Leicester. I must thank Simon Fletcher, Michelle Tilling and their colleagues at Sutton Publishing for the valuable assistance and advice offered while producing this book. My thanks go also to the individuals and organisations that have permitted me to reproduce photographs and illustrations from their collections. I have made every effort to identify and contact all current copyright owners for their permission to reproduce the photographs and illustrations contained in this volume, but in some cases this was not possible. In these cases I have attributed the images to their current owners. If I have omitted any person or organisation from the following list, I apologise and suggest that they contact me immediately through the publisher so that a full and correct acknowledgement can be given in a future reprint. My thanks go to Barry and Stephanie Gallant, Sheila Allen, Richard Tacon, Glenda Tooke, Margaret and John White, Val and Gem Cole, David Riley, Deanna Lewis, Andrew Fakes, Eddie Bates, Carrie Spencer, Maureen Turner and local historian Colin Tooke, for permission to reproduce photographs from their private albums; to Archant Norfolk Limited, Leicestershire County Record Office and the Leicester University Archives Department for permission to use photographs and illustrations from their archive collections and extracts from the *Great Yarmouth Mercury*, the *Eastern Daily Press* and the Leicester University Student magazine *Ripple*. I also thank the Heritage House Group for permission to replicate postcards from English Life Publications.

I dedicate this volume to the memory of my parents, Raymond and Gertrude Miller, my grandparents, Walter and Nora Miller and Arthur and Edith Cole, and to my many uncles, aunts and cousins who played an important part in my early life.

Opening Gambit

'Memories are made of this', Dean Martin, 1956

This book is about the 1950s, a decade that I remember with some clarity and a period in my life that I look back on with great affection. It was a decade that began with austerity but ended in relative prosperity, a time when the Coronation gave people the hope of a new Elizabethan revival, a period in which nuclear war with Russia was a distinct possibility and the debacle of Suez marked the end of Britain as a leading power in world politics. It was a decade in which young people, better off financially than their parents' generation, developed a culture of their own, allegedly based around rock 'n' roll and coffee bars. I have no intention of claiming that life was better back then, because for many people it was not. Everyday life was certainly much harder in a country slowly recovering from a major war. The technology that we now take for granted had yet to make a significant impact on our daily lives, both at work and at play. As was the case with my family, men went to work, but, out of necessity, most working class women stayed at home to bring up their children and do housework – those numerous exacting and time-consuming chores that have now been made simpler by the availability of washing machines, tumble-driers, refrigerators, freezers and ready made meals. The 1950s may not have been better but they were certainly different, and it is some of those differences that I hope to describe in this book. I intend to outline my own background based mainly on my personal experiences and memories of the 1950s, a decade covering all of my teenage years, my transition from boy to man, and my progression through Great Yarmouth Grammar School to university in Leicester. For me it was a time of excitement, of discovery, a time when things were new and my adult life stretched before me.

It is also mainly about Norfolk, the village of Rollesby where I grew up, its neighbouring villages, Great Yarmouth and Norwich, with some brief references to my initial experiences in the city of Leicester. It is about people, in particular my close-knit family in Rollesby and Yarmouth; my village, school and student friends; and the rural and urban communities where I spent my early life. Where possible I have supported these memories by consulting my family and friends, and by referring to contemporary newspapers, especially the *Yarmouth Mercury*, the *Eastern Daily Press* and the Leicester University student magazine, *Ripple*. But primarily it is about the ways in which ordinary people entertained themselves or were entertained by others during their leisure time in the 1950s, those periods in the day away from paid employment, housework or, in my case, school and college. To be more precise,

The end of youth. Mother, father and me on a rare excursion to Rollesby Church, 1962. I lost weight living on a poor student diet. My parents, on the other hand, were good adverts for Macmillan's Britain. (Author's Collection)

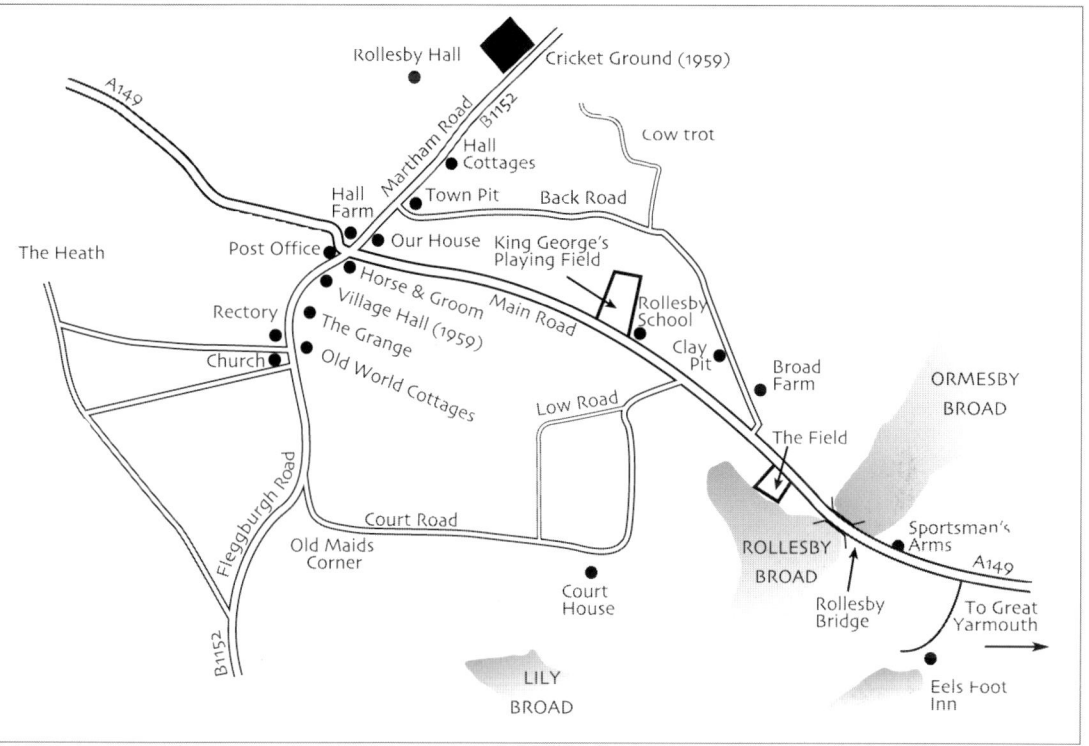

Map of Rollesby.

it is about the many ways in which I, a Norfolk teenager, filled my spare time with my parents and friends at home, in Rollesby and the villages of the Broadland 'Fleggs', the urban environments of Yarmouth and Norwich, and in my first year at university in Leicester.

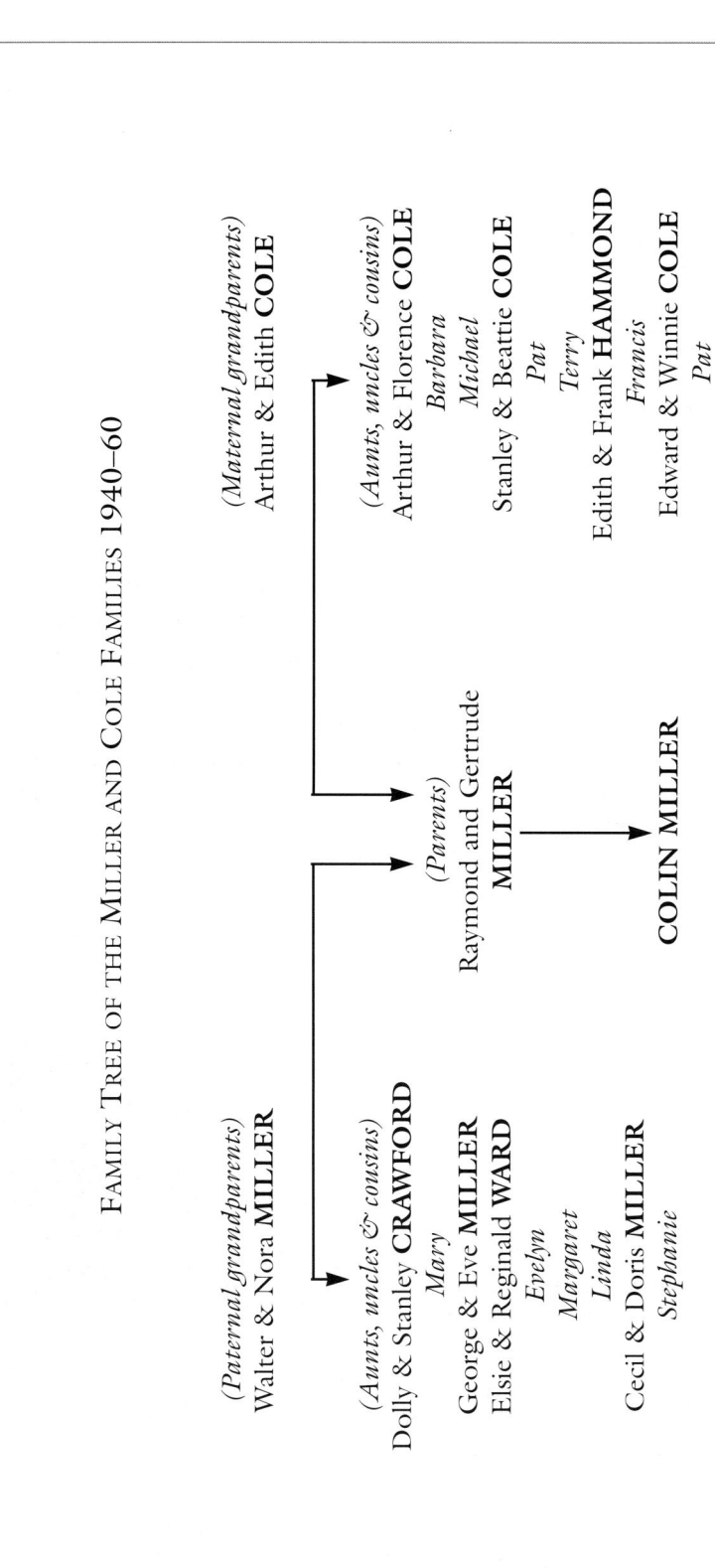

FAMILY TREE OF THE MILLER AND COLE FAMILIES 1940–60

(Paternal grandparents)
Walter & Nora **MILLER**

(Maternal grandparents)
Arthur & Edith **COLE**

(Aunts, uncles & cousins)
Dolly & Stanley **CRAWFORD**
  Mary
George & Eve **MILLER**
Elsie & Reginald **WARD**
  Evelyn
  Margaret
  Linda
Cecil & Doris **MILLER**
  Stephanie

(Parents)
Raymond and Gertrude
MILLER

COLIN MILLER

(Aunts, uncles & cousins)
Arthur & Florence **COLE**
  Barbara
  Michael
Stanley & Beattie **COLE**
  Pat
  Terry
Edith & Frank **HAMMOND**
  Francis
Edward & Winnie **COLE**
  Pat
  Tony
Doris & Billy **PARNELL**
  Deanna
Bob & Doris **COLE**
  Margaret
  Val

The family tree of the Millers and the Coles.

1

Beginnings

The Village of Rollesby

'The story of my life', Michael Holiday, 1958

I was born on 5 August 1940 at Rollesby, a small Broadland village in the county of Norfolk, 8 miles west of the seaside town of Great Yarmouth and 16 miles north-east of Norwich. Rollesby is located on the east to west route of the A149 (known locally as the Main Road), linking Rollesby to the villages of Ormesby and Repps, and the north to south B1152 between Martham and Fleggburgh; one of a small group of farming villages in the north of Broadland Norfolk forming an area called the Fleggs. To the east, the village is bounded by three large conjoined freshwater broads – the Rollesby, Ormesby and Filby Broads – collectively known as the Trinity Broad. For the next nineteen years I lived with my parents, Raymond and Gertrude Miller, in a small rented semi-detached house on the northern section of the B1152 that was and still is known as the Martham Road.

Our family home was a small, bay-fronted semi-detached house that was built in the 1920s and contained two reception rooms (a living room and a front room), a

Martham Road, Rollesby, 1951, with our semi-detached house on the right. Traffic was so light that children could play games along the road in relative safety. (Richard Tacon)

Rollesby post office, 1951. I regularly visited the family-run post office for coffee, cards and conversation, and, in my later teens, to cadge cigarettes from my Aunt Doris Miller. (Sheila Allen)

scullery, two double bedrooms and a box room. Normal daily life was spent in the aptly named living room, which served as both sitting room and dining room. In the 1940s it also served as the kitchen, as the living room at that time was equipped with a large black iron cooking range. In 1947 my father removed the range and replaced it with a modern open fireplace. A new electric oven was put in the scullery, which, up until then, had been mainly used as a laundry room. Despite being equipped with the best furniture and our well-polished upright piano, the front room was used only for special occasions and family parties. My parents slept in one of the double bedrooms – the other bedroom was used as visitor accommodation and, occasionally, for storing apples picked from the trees in our garden. The box room became my teenage refuge. We had neither a bathroom nor an indoor toilet. Until 1952, our drinking water was obtained from a well in the landlord's garden and stored in enamel buckets in the scullery. In 1952 we were connected to a mains water supply via a single cold-water tap in the scullery. The only toilet was an outdoor bucket lavatory, which was emptied every fortnight into a container lorry supplied by the local district council. Outside there was a relatively large productive vegetable garden with a greengage, a bullace and three apple trees.

Both my parents came from large families, a relatively common occurrence fifty or so years ago. On my father's side, my Rollesby grandparents, Walter and Nora Miller, had six children; four boys and two girls: Dorothy (Dolly), George, Elsie, Cecil, Raymond (my father) and Kenneth. Kenneth unfortunately died of diphtheria in infancy during the 1920s. My maternal grandparents, Arthur and Edith Cole, lived at 12 North Market Road in Great Yarmouth and also had a large family consisting of four boys and three girls: Arthur, Stanley, Edith, Edward, Doris, Gertrude (my mother) and Robert (Bob). By the 1950s, all my aunts and uncles were married and most had children of a similar age to me. Apart from Grandfather Cole, who died when I was two, my surviving grandparents and many of my aunts, uncles and cousins lived locally and much of my teenage leisure time was spent in their company. My Miller grandparents lived at and ran the Rollesby Post Office and Stores, which was located at the crossing of the Main Road and the B1152, a short walk away from our house. In 1950, when Grandmother Miller developed breast cancer and was forced to retire, they moved to Hall Cottages, a black and white mock-Tudor semi-detached residence on the Martham Road, where they remained until she died in 1957. The management of the post office was passed on to my Uncle Cecil Miller and his wife, Doris.

Both families, the Millers and the Coles, were working class, although my two grandfathers, and most of my uncles, were tradesmen rather than labourers – Grandfather Cole was a tin-plate worker and Grandfather Miller, a carpenter and wheelwright. After completing his apprenticeship, Grandfather Miller joined the army as a regular soldier and served in the Middle East and Ireland during and after the First World War. On leaving the army in the 1920s, as well as moving into the post office, he took over the organisation of a small market garden close to Rollesby Broad (known to the family as The Field) where he also established a base for a small building firm which he continued to run until the mid-1950s, a notice on the gate proudly advertising 'W.J. Miller, builder'.

In 1931, my father joined grandfather's firm and served his apprenticeship as a bricklayer. In 1936, at the age of twenty, he moved to the Midlands with my mother's brothers Arthur, Stanley and Bob in search of employment in the manufacturing industry and on the building sites of Birmingham, returning to Rollesby at the outbreak of war in 1939. For the next seven years, my father spent most of his time away from home, initially as a member of a construction gang

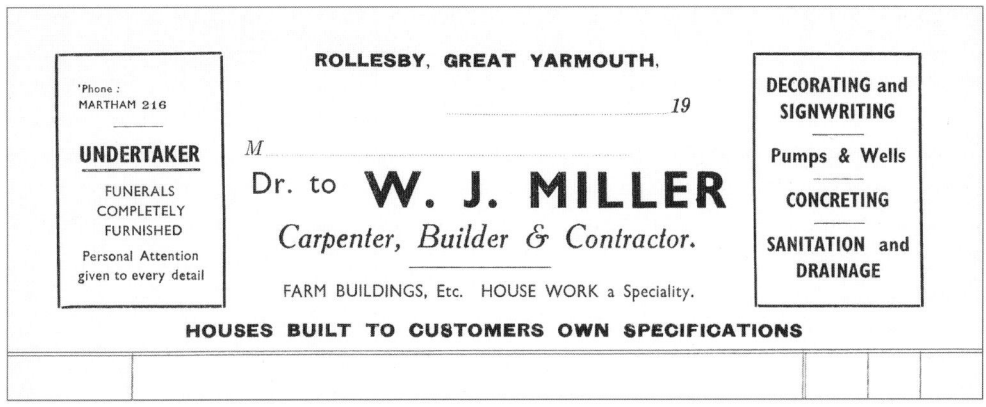

The Miller family gathering for tea on the lawn at Hall Cottages, 1953. Back row: my father, Uncles Cecil and George, Grandfather Miller. Front row: Aunt Eve, my mother, Cousin Stephanie, Grandmother Miller, Aunt Doris. (Author's Collection)

building airfields for the RAF and then on war service with the Royal Engineers in Italy and Austria. On his demobilisation in January 1947, he resumed working in the building trade as a contract bricklayer and plasterer. During the 1950s, mother followed the then socially accepted role for women of housewife and parent, which was a hard and time-consuming occupation but one that she relished. To help with the family budget, she often took seasonal part-time labouring work in the fields and market gardens of Rollesby, and as a cleaner at a Martham boatyard and the Caister Holiday Camp. Nevertheless, she always considered that her primary function was to look after the house and her family, a role she discharged so efficiently that when I eventually left home I discovered I was not properly prepared for living on my own.

For mother, father and me, my father's demobilisation in 1947 marked the start of a normal family life, a full and active life that still remains vivid in my memory. Perhaps 1947 also marked the beginning of normality in the social life of our village as the trappings of war were dismantled and the servicemen and women returned home. Luckily, wartime had not interrupted my schooling. In 1945, at just five years of age, I joined the infant class at the Rollesby County Primary School and began an education which, in 1951, led to success in the Common Entrance Examination (the eleven-plus) and a place at the Great Yarmouth Grammar School for boys. My constant companions throughout the 1950s were Tony, Tim and Richard. Tony, a farm worker's son who lived at Chapel Cottages on the Back Road in Rollesby, was my best friend at primary school and remained a friend after I started my schooling at Yarmouth. I met Tim, who hailed from the coastal village of Hemsby, at grammar school and, as we came from similar rural backgrounds, we formed a strong friendship that lasted until university and beyond. Richard was a gentleman farmer's son and, as such, would not normally be able to develop friendships with the sons of bricklayers. Nevertheless, a strong bond had long existed between our two families ever since my great-grandmother was employed for most of her working life as housekeeper to Richard's grandfather and his family.

In the 1950s, Rollesby was a small self-contained rural community of 500 or so people, most of whom were employed in agriculture and other rural or service occupations. Most of our daily needs were provided for by four small shops and numerous travelling vans which visited the village on a regular basis to sell and deliver coal, meat, fish, bread, milk and general groceries. What was not available in Rollesby could usually be obtained in one of the adjacent Flegg villages (Martham, Fleggburgh, Ormesby, Filby and Repps) a short cycle ride away, or at Great Yarmouth, the nearest market town. Martham, a larger village than Rollesby and 1½ miles distant, possessed a bank, a doctor's surgery, a hardware business, two butchers, a baker, and a barber's shop, in addition to the usual general grocery stores. In most of these villages, communal leisure activities were organised by village-based clubs, societies and church organisations, held at the local public house, church rooms, village hall or primary school, or on a designated recreation field, and were usually very well supported.

A meeting of the Coles at a wedding, 1960. Grandma Cole with some of my aunts, uncles and cousins. (Author's Collection)

Great Yarmouth, the closest town to Rollesby, was thirty minutes away by bus – a red number 5 bus belonging to the Eastern Counties Omnibus Company that travelled hourly along a circular route from Yarmouth to Norwich and back. At weekends in my late teens, I regularly journeyed to Yarmouth alone or with my friends not only to visit my mother's family and to shop at Yarmouth's market and department stores, but also to make use of its entertainment facilities – its sporting venues, cinemas, theatres and dance halls. In the summer, Yarmouth provided additional attractions via its role as a popular seaside holiday resort. In my late teens those attractions were often female.

In October 1959 I left behind my comfortable existence in Rollesby to study for a degree at Leicester University. For a working class Norfolk country boy, the city of Leicester and its university were both exciting yet daunting places. Leicester in the 1950s was a bustling, prosperous, industrial Midlands city whose wealth was based on the production of hosiery, knitted goods and footwear. The population of about 300,000 was predominantly indigenous white working class, together with small but rapidly growing communities of Eastern European, Caribbean and Asian descent. At the heart of Leicester stood a symbolic Clock Tower around which was located the main shopping area, a wholesale fruit, vegetable and fish market, and most of Leicester's entertainment facilities.

The university, founded in 1921, was situated on a site between the London and Welford roads adjacent to Victoria Park, close to the centre of Leicester. The sombre main buildings were formerly used as a mental hospital and had been

The main Fielding Johnson building, Leicester University, as it was in the 1950s. University was a big step for a working class country boy like me. (Leicester University Archives)

The Percy Gee building, opened in 1958, was the centre for most student recreational activities. Some of its social attractions proved to be a great distraction from my studies. (© English Life Publications/Heritage House Group Ltd)

adapted to create administrative offices, a library, lecture theatres and tutorial rooms. During the 1950s new buildings had been added including, in 1958, the Percy Gee building that housed the offices of the Leicester University Students' Union and various recreational facilities including a bar, bookshop, undergraduate and postgraduate common rooms, dining hall, games rooms and a squash court. Apart from occasional forays into the main university campus for lectures or to use the library, the Percy Gee was the centre for my student life at Leicester and the building in which I spent most of my time, engaging in activities and projects not always to do with my formal education. My knowledge of the city of Leicester was limited to those recreational and leisure facilities in the city centre, especially the location of numerous public houses, eating places, cinemas and dance halls, and the Leicester City football and rugby grounds at Filbert Street and Welford Road respectively. In 1959, as a first-year freshman, I was allocated a room in Southmead House, an annexe of the university's Beaumont Hall of Residence but, thereafter, my accommodation was a succession of damp and dingy rented flats.

Throughout all of the 1950s, during my years as a teenager in Rollesby and as a newly installed student at Leicester, I lived a full and active life at work and in my leisure hours. Despite the absence of multi-channelled television, computers, iPods, DVD players and their like, I was hardly ever bored, even as a moderately rebellious teenager. As I recollect, my parents, family or friends were never bored either, filling their time away from work with a variety of activities and entertainments many of which have become less popular or have even disappeared as new technology, particularly television, has come to dominate most of our leisure time. The following chapters are an account of how I, together with my family and friends, filled our spare hours and days during the 1950s, a decade of transition not only socially, economically, morally and technologically, but also in leisure time pursuits.

2

Leisure Time at Home

PLAYING GAMES

'Nothin' to do', Michael Holliday, 1956

Throughout my teenage years, I cannot recollect a time when I was not busy. Even when my work was finished and it was time to relax, I found plenty to do. Mother often complained that I was 'always on the go'. At home, I filled my spare time with hobbies, drawing, painting, playing cards, reading, listening to the radio or records on my record player, watching television, strumming my ukulele and guitar, and playing games. I played games by myself, with friends or as part of a team; I played them in the house, the garden, at school, the public house, a village hall or at a playing field. I challenged myself, an opponent or the members of an opposing team in games of all descriptions – traditional games including those played with dominoes, draughts and cards, commercially produced games that were bought as boxed sets, cricket, football and other sporting events, as well as variations on games that were our own inventions.

For many young people, leisure time at home involved playing games against their parents and siblings. Being an only child with busy parents, playing games with my mother or father was limited to those odd and often rare occasions in the evening when they had some time to spare. With my village friends, Richard and Tony, I preferred to be outside exploring the countryside or playing endless cricket and football matches in a meadow or at the recreation field. Playing games at home was for dark winter nights, periods of bad weather, or those rare interludes of boredom when I had nothing to do. With my parents engaged on other tasks, I was frequently left to play on my own, solving puzzles and competing in games against myself. In my early teens I spent hours playing indoor cricket with two shiny metal dice, usually as an imaginary game between England and Australia. At the start of the game, I wrote the names of eleven players for both teams in an old exercise book, players whose names were well known to a young cricket fanatic – Hutton, Compton, Washbrook, Edrich, Evans, Laker and Bedser versus Barnes, Morris, Bradman, Hassett, Miller and Lindwall, to name but a few. England always batted first. Each player in turn was deemed to be in bat. On the faces of one dice were engraved 1, 1, 2, 4, 6 and 'Howzat'. The number rolled with this dice was the batsman's score for each ball and this was recorded in the exercise book, unless the result was 'Howzat'. Then, the second dice was rolled to determine the result of that appeal. On each of its faces were inscribed 'not out', 'bowled', 'lbw', 'caught', 'run out' and 'stumped'. Once a player was out, it was the next player's turn to bat, and so on until all eleven in the side had batted. Then it was the turn of Australia. No matter how hard I tried or even cheated, I could never always contrive an England win.

I loved puzzles of all kinds – I separated bent nails that were linked together in contorted shapes, I moved small plastic squares inscribed with the numbers 1 to 15 around a 4 by 4 grid trying to get them in numerical order, I tried solving the crosswords in our daily newspaper. To be precise, I solved the day's easy crossword and failed on the rest. Mother and I loved jigsaws and so we both spent many evenings joining jigsaw pieces on a tray, sometimes working at the same puzzle, at other times on a puzzle of our own. Corners first, the straight bits next and then sort out the middle – usually a 500-piece jigsaw and a 1,000-piece jigsaw at Christmas. Sometimes our jigsaws were new, at other times they were bought at a village jumble sale, though all too often the latter were missing pieces or even contained pieces from another puzzle. Sometimes the trays we used were too small to accommodate a completed puzzle, a frustrating problem until my father brought home a large architect's drawing board for us to use. Most games in the garden involved a ball of one sort or another, especially when I played by myself. I

practiced cricket and football against a wall, setting myself targets or trying to break a personal record. How many times can I catch a ball bounced off a wall or hit a wicket drawn in chalk on that wall or trap a football kicked against the wall? I tried wiggling my hips in an attempt to perfect my technique with a hula-hoop. When no-one was free to join in with me, I even played ping-pong by myself on the dining table against the living room wall.

I enjoyed playing games against my friends, parents and grandparents, mostly paper-and-pencil, card and board games. At home, my father taught me Noughts & Crosses and Hangman which we usually played on the back of old envelopes, and with my school friends I played Battleships – a coordinate game played either on a square grid drawn on a piece of plain paper or sometimes on large squared graph paper smuggled out of maths classes. On wet days, Richard and I competed in endless games of Dover Patrol, a commercially produced board game for two players that simulated naval warfare. When not otherwise occupied, my father was happy to play me at cards or any game that had a sporting connection. In my younger years we engaged in frantic games of blow football, eventually progressing to ping-pong on the dining table. In my teens we played highly competitive games of billiards on his small portable billiard table, watched over carefully by my mother in an attempt to protect her ornaments. In the mid-1950s, I was addicted to the football game, Subutteo. With my Rollesby friends, Tony, Richard and Dick, we competed against each other in our own mini-league, fielding personal teams with our own team colours selected from a range offered by Subutteo. As I remember, my team wore shirts with orange and black stripes.

By the 1950s, I had progressed beyond snakes and ladders, Ludo, tiddlywinks and draughts. At thirteen years of age my passion was chess, a game taught to me by Grandfather Miller, who considered himself to be an expert chess player. We regularly played hard-fought matches in his office when he was supposed to be working at his papers. Many boys played 'travelling' chess on mini-pegboards with small plastic pieces, small enough to be concealed in a pocket. At Yarmouth Grammar School, Tim and I played travelling chess before and after school, in the long lunch breaks, and even under the desk as an antidote to boring lessons. Some of the more serious players recorded their moves in a notebook, apparently to study at a later date – to my mind a pointless activity. Although there were local chess clubs and even a chess league, I preferred playing grandfather and Tim. At university, I discovered my limitations when I was soundly beaten by a post-graduate student who was an international chess player, an experience made worse by the fact that he was playing seven others at the same time, spending ten seconds at each board before moving on to the next, in the process beating all eight competitors with consummate ease.

At family get-togethers and parties, we often played noisy but highly competitive games – mostly commercially produced shop-bought games. Grandmother Miller was addicted to Lexicon, a word-game not unlike Scrabble but played with cards, and tea with Grandmother Miller often finished with a lively game of Lexicon. At Aunt Dolly Crawford's in Martham we always played Beetle, a game where the aim was to win all the parts of that insect by rolling different numbers with a dice. Beetle was so popular in the 1950s that some village halls organised Beetle drives as an alternative to whist drives. My mother's favourite game was Pit, a card game based on the stock market, in which up to seven competitors noisily swapped cards in an attempt to collect a complete set of one commodity or another, while trying to avoid two penalty cards – the Bull and the Bear. This was a game where a poker face was important, as it was necessary not to let opponents know when you were swapping either the Bull or the Bear. Grandma Cole was never successful at this game as she always laughed hysterically when she received either card. From that moment on, any exchange of cards with her was deliberately avoided. On his return from war service, my father introduced us to a game that he regularly played in the army called Housey-Housey, the game that is now known as Bingo. We also had a Monopoly set, a game invented in America during the 1930s and marketed by Waddington that became extremely popular immediately after the Second World War. Towards the end of our family parties, mother often suggested a game of Monopoly but I cannot ever remember a game being finished.

HOBBIES & PASTIMES

'Among my souvenirs', Connie Francis, 1960

By the early 1950s, I had put away most of my childish toys and games to fill my leisure hours with hobbies that mostly involved collecting or making things. My bedroom companions of infancy, my teddy and panda (the latter battered with its head held on by a safety pin) had long been relegated to the garden shed, my fort and tin soldiers lay discarded in my cupboard, my cap guns had shot their last imaginary Indian and Snakes & Ladders and Ludo had lost their appeal. Encouraged by my form master at Yarmouth Grammar School, I filled my leisure time with activities designed to increase my general knowledge or to develop my practical skills.

GRAMMAR SCHOOL BOYS' HOBBIES. VARIED EXHIBITS ON SHOW

Visitors to Yarmouth Grammar School's hobbies exhibition in the school hall on Saturday afternoon saw a vast number of exhibits ranging from stamp collections and Meccano models to canoes and model aeroplanes. Mr R. Teasdale who organised the exhibition told a reporter that it was the first exhibition to be held for three years. He said that the boys were asked for exhibits about two weeks previously and in that time most of them had been made.

It was obvious from the large display of exhibits that the boys had put a considerable amount of time into preparing their work. Several of the exhibits, notably a canoe and a wireless set, were first class . . . There were about 2,000 stamps on show. They were prepared by I. Tosh, B. Reid, D. Canham, J. Ward and D. Emmerson. The mathematical exhibits were made under the supervision of Mr T.E. Stafford, the mathematics master. They included the five regular Platonic Polyhedron, ruled surfaces and wired models. Some photographic exhibits were prepared by C. Tooke and J. Lincoln. N. Hardy made a model yacht and there were three model houses constructed by R. Clayton, L. Bewley and J. Pereira, several model aeroplanes, including one reputed to be capable of travelling at 60mph. A film show was given by I. Tilley.

Yarmouth Mercury, 2 April 1954

My favourite hobby was stamp collecting. My collection was based initially on a blue and gold album that my father gave me, containing stamps that he had collected during his childhood. Most weeks I purchased packets of used stamps from F.W. Woolworth & Co. in Great Yarmouth to add to the collection. On a school trip to Windsor in 1953, I was amazed to discover a shop close by the castle that sold stamps solely for collectors, new and used stamps from the Commonwealth and many foreign countries. I spent a long time in that shop looking longingly at the stamps and eventually spent 2s, virtually all the spending money I had saved for the outing, on a £1 King George VI used stamp from the unified countries of Kenya, Uganda and Tanganyika. I was convinced at the time that a £1 stamp would have the same rarity value as a Victorian penny black. To me £1 was a fortune. Stamp collecting became even more popular with the Coronation of Queen Elizabeth II. Grandmother Miller arranged for me to receive a day of issue cover for the first Elizabethan stamps, a red 2½d and a green 1½d. Uncle George Miller was a keen stamp collector and in his spare time ran a stamp approval business. As a London-based branch manager in the Bank of India, he had access to stamps from all over the world, especially stamps from Asia, which he bought from the bank and resold by mail order. When he eventually gave up this business, he gave the remnants of his stock books and a large collection of foreign stamps to me. I was very proud of my collection, which contained many thousands of stamps from all over the world. During the dark winter evenings I often looked through my collection, searching for the countries in my battered world atlas and learning a great deal about that country from the pictures and designs on their stamps.

I also had a small collection of cigarette cards, given to me by my grandfather. Many of my friends collected, traded, swapped, flicked and even gambled with cigarette cards. Despite the fact that most brands had ceased to include cards in their packets during the 1940s, there were still many cards in general circulation, mainly odd cards or incomplete sets. Aunt Muriel Allen (a distant relative) was a heavy smoker of Turf cigarettes, which continued to include picture cards as part of the internal packaging of its cigarette boxes, one card in a packet of ten and two in a packet of twenty. I regularly visited and even pestered her in my quest to collect these cards, particularly those from various sports series, usually of fifty cards each, that depicted many of my contemporary British sporting heroes: footballers Stanley Matthews and Tom Finney, the test cricketers Len Hutton, Dennis Compton, Cyril Washbrook and Godfrey Evans, boxer Bruce Woodcock and the jockey Gordon Richards to name but a few. During the 1950s, Brook Bond began to include picture cards in its packets of tea, but these didn't have the same appeal as cigarette cards.

I undoubtedly inherited my collecting habit from my Miller grandparents. My grandmother collected brass ornaments and blue and white porcelain, especially porcelain decorated in the Chinese willow pattern, which she bought in local shops, house auctions or at the weekly Thursday market sale in the nearby village of Acle. Every surface in her spotlessly tidy home was covered with well-polished brasses and blue and white ornaments and plates. When we had tea at her house we ate off and drank out of blue and white crockery. When she died in 1957 and her collection was auctioned, mother often stated that she had overheard a London dealer say that my grandfather would not be so pleased with the proceeds if he knew how cheaply the collection was being sold. Grandfather Miller was a hoarder and collected anything of interest which he kept in his 'office', a large wooden shed in his garden. A power cable from the house to the shed provided the energy for a light and a socket for his electric fire. On one side of the shed numerous box files were placed on three shelves and contained the paperwork for his building firm and for his role as village Churchwarden and Parish Clerk, and against the window stood a desk and a swivel chair. On the desk and scattered around the office was his collection of objects of interest. I spent many happy hours with grandfather sitting on a stool in his office looking at his objects and listening to his tales.

On top of the desk was a large blotter, an ornamental bone-handled letter opener and a collection of paperweights, many from local suppliers of building materials. I still possess one of his paperweights, an advertising gift from A & W Cushion, timber importers of Norwich. Numerous Toby jugs and pewter mugs held his pens, pencils and paintbrushes, and a wooden rack was filled with envelopes and writing paper. Under the desk he had a collection of bayonets and brass artillery shell cases salvaged from the First World War. His redundant Second World War air-raid warden's helmet and gas mask hung on the back of the door beneath an assortment of hats, caps and coats. The desk drawers were filled not only with office materials and stationery but also with personal memorabilia, photograph albums and scrapbooks. An old oak cabinet in one corner held his birds' egg collection of two hundred or more blown eggs contained in a dozen glass-covered display cases and numerous cigar boxes, together with various books on birds and birds' eggs, which I read avidly. After grandmother died, he moved back to Rollesby post office to live with Uncle Cecil Miller and Aunt Doris. When he moved, he gave me a large oak sideboard from his living room and the birds' egg collection, much to my mother's disgust. She did not approve of the collection, saying vociferously that every egg represented a destroyed bird. At the earliest opportunity and without grandfather's knowledge she arranged for the collection to be sold. Although I was a keen bird's-nester, seeking out nests and following with interest the progress of the chicks inside, I was never tempted to become an egg collector.

Being a country boy, it was inevitable that I should develop an interest in the natural world. I collected beetles and caterpillars, created a wormery and unintentionally suffocated butterflies and moths in a jar. I pressed leaves and flowers between the pages of a book, baked conkers for the autumn conker championships, ate hazelnuts and blackberries from the hedgerows as well as collecting pan-sized field mushrooms from the nearby meadows for my mother to fry. I watched with interest the animals and birds around me through grandfather's opera glasses, and peered at insects with a magnifying glass that Grandmother Miller gave me. I discovered, with some delight, that the magnifying glass could also focus the rays from the sun causing paper to burn, matches to spontaneously ignite and unsuspecting school friends to experience pain. To further my interest in nature, my parents bought me a small microscope with a dozen or more mounted specimens on slides. I also produced my own specimens by sandwiching various objects of interest between two glass blocks – the wings and legs of a fly, a strand of human hair, sugar and salt crystals, dirty water from the rainwater butt and anything small enough that caught my fancy.

At other times I made collections of seashells from the beaches at Hemsby and Great Yarmouth, lucky stones, beer bottle tops, tobacco tins that seemed always to retain that sweet smell of tobacco, matchbox labels and cigarette packets. I even made lists of car registration numbers. I caught butterflies in nets and gathered frogspawn and tadpoles in jam jars from the Town Pit, a pond at the end of our road. I once incurred the wrath of my father by emptying my collection of tadpoles into one of our outside rainwater butts. I was fascinated watching them wiggling about among the mosquito larvae. I cannot remember what eventually happened to them but it is unlikely that any emergent frog would have been able to escape from the butt. In our early teens, my friend Richard and I collected Dinky racing cars – including models painted in the logos of Talbot, Alfa Romeo, Cooper, Ferrari and Maserati – which we raced on a track that we built in the attic of his home at the Grange.

Everybody collected personal memorabilia – items, ephemera, photographs and writings relating to special times, places, events or people, which they kept in a journal, album, diary or scrapbook. My cousin Deanna collected the autographs of 'famous' entertainers, which she kept in a small multi-coloured album. In the summer she spent long hours outside the stage doors of Great Yarmouth's many theatres in the hope of obtaining autographs from the stars appearing at their summer shows. Her favourite acquisition was the autograph of Roger Moore, a trophy obtained as he tried in vain to remain anonymous while waiting for Dorothy Squires to finish a concert. My autograph album was more prosaic and contained mainly poems, drawings, personal messages and signatures inscribed by various members of my family and school friends. It did, however, contain a signed photograph of Max Miller whom I had met accidentally outside the Regal Theatre in Great Yarmouth. Out of curiosity, I had joined an excited group of people surrounding a flashily dressed man who was handing out publicity photographs. It was only later, on inspecting the photograph, that I discovered he was the well-known comedian Max Miller. Grandfather Miller had an album commemorating his time in the army which contained family prayers, verses and good wishes for his safety, drawings and cartoons, comments from his comrades, photographs of grandfather taken on active service, paper ephemera including his discharge notice, and two photographs labelled 'Taken from the pocket of a dead Hun'. Grandmother Miller had an album of postcards that had been sent to her by friends and family, including a number of embroidered silk cards with motifs relating to events and regiments of the First World War.

Scrapbooks were popular, usually consisting of cuttings from magazines and newspapers. I made numerous scrapbooks. One contained pictures and articles relating to the Royal Family, another photographs of jet aircraft, particularly of the Comet jet airliner. One friend made a scrapbook consisting entirely of the obituaries of famous film stars. Most people possessed personal photograph albums that contained both professionally produced studio portraits and their own snapshots of family members past and present, weddings and christenings, which were usually brought out for inspection when visitors came to tea. For my thirteenth birthday I was given a small box camera, but photography proved to be far too expensive to become a regular hobby. Uncle George Miller had a Leica camera and financed his hobby by taking and selling his photographs, usually studies of flowers and plants that he sold through an agent to botanic and gardening magazines. One of his local projects was a series of scenic photographs of Rollesby which were produced as postcards and sold at the post office.

As we were without a home telephone, letter writing was our main form of communication in the 1950s. I frequently sent letters to family and friends written with a fountain pen on Basildon Bond plain paper. I even had a French pen pal. Many organisations and schools found pen pals for their members and pupils, many of them from overseas. Some of my friends wrote regularly to more than one correspondent. Mother always ensured that I sent 'Thank you' letters after every Christmas and birthday. At university, I wrote a four-page letter to my mother every Sunday morning and she wrote a reply every Wednesday, a habit that persisted until we both acquired telephones in the 1970s. Writing in a diary was also a relatively popular activity, possibly encouraged by the radio programme *Mrs Dale's Diary* and the poignant wartime diary of Anne Frank. A few of my cousins kept daily diaries and every evening wrote in it a record of their day's activities. I was usually given a diary at Christmas and, every January, I began a record of my daily experiences. However, by February the entries became shorter, or were even forgotten, and by March my diary keeping had usually ceased.

For as long as I can remember, we always had a pet of some description. Mother was keen that I should learn about animals and understand how to look after them. We always had a cat, usually one rescued from the wild. My father was an enthusiastic cat fancier and spent hours trying to persuade one or other of the unkempt animals at the Field or from the farm opposite to leave its wild ways and adopt a life of luxury in our house. Occasionally he was successful and, as a consequence, during my childhood, we had a continuous succession of cats – first Vicky, who was succeeded by Whiskey, then Smokey and Tinkle, and eventually Granny and Herbert. None of these cats had the luxury of food from a tin. They were expected to survive on bread soaked in milk, the leavings from our dinners and whatever they were able to catch. Occasionally, mother bought cat meat from the butcher, a minced-up concoction of offal, fat, skin and odd scraps of meat that the butcher was unable to sell. This she boiled in a saucepan on the stove, filling the whole house with an obnoxious smell. For the cats it was a treat. When Grandmother Miller died we inherited her dog, a slightly overweight brown and white spaniel called Rover. Rover and I were great friends, as I had been entrusted with exercising him ever since he was a puppy. This usually involved chasing games along the tracks and meadows near to Rollesby Hall and tempting him to retrieve sticks from impossible places such as the middle of the Town Pit, a bramble bush or a patch of mud. Although Rover was great company, he had one very bad habit – he made smells. One memorable day when the vicar made a visit, Rover surpassed himself by making the smell of all smells. How the vicar, mother and I continued to make small talk in an atmosphere reminiscent of the school chemistry laboratory I am not sure, but the vicar very quickly made his excuses and left. As far as I can recall, thanks to Rover, we were never visited again.

Mother was a great animal lover. She kept cats, a dog, chickens and rabbits. She once had a pig and cried when it died. (Author's Collection)

Apart from Uncle Cecil who kept dogs (a succession of Black Labradors) few of my other relatives had either a cat or a dog, especially my urban relatives. Grandma Cole had a ginger cat, but not out of choice, as it was a surprise gift from my mother to keep her company when she was alone. Although she cared for the cat, spoiling it often with fish scraps from the market, life with grandma was not easy. I frequently wondered how the cat coped, especially with its toilet, living in an urban environment surrounded by factories, busy roads, buildings and houses with their small backyards mostly covered in concrete. Most of my Yarmouth relatives preferred to keep birds, a canary or budgerigar, repeating phrases at it in a parrot-like

Rover and me, 1953. Rover was allowed to run free around the village and nobody seemed to mind. (Author's Collection)

voice in the hope that it might learn to talk. As well as keeping a caged budgerigar in his living room, Uncle Billy Parnell, a member of the Yarmouth and Gorleston Cage Bird Society, bred canaries in his backyard at Audley Street in Great Yarmouth. He also possessed a cage of finches, as by crossing a canary with a goldfinch he could produce a bird called a mule, which looked like a canary but was an excellent songbird. This was a common practice among some breeders, including Uncle Billy, but one discouraged and considered unethical by the Cage Bird Society. I was intrigued by his collection of birds but mother again disapproved, asserting that birds should fly free and not be housed in cages. Pigeons were less popular locally than the traditional Norfolk canary or budgerigar, although there was an active pigeon flying club in Ormesby. Some children kept white mice in a box but nobody that I knew possessed a hamster, guinea pig or gerbil. We had rabbits which we housed in a hutch by the hedge. During the summer I was responsible for collecting their food from the hedgerows, mostly dandelion leaves and cow parsley, and for cleaning out the hutches. In the autumn they were sold at Acle sale. Grandmother Miller had a tortoise, which lived on the lawn in summer and disappeared in winter. One winter it disappeared for good.

ARTS & CRAFTS

'Mona Lisa', Conway Twitty, 1959

As a teenager I enjoyed painting and drawing at an age when most children had put away their pencils and crayons to explore other opportunities. Encouraged by my grandfather, who was a good amateur artist, and Mr Excell, the art master at Great Yarmouth Grammar School, a fresh-faced young man with the naïve enthusiasm of a newly qualified teacher, I derived much pleasure from developing good technical skills in pen or pencil drawing and watercolour painting. In my bedroom an old biscuit tin held my collection of lead pencils, pens, paintbrushes of different sizes, bottles of red, blue, green and black ink, my treasured Windsor & Newton watercolour paint box, sticks of charcoal and numerous tubes and spare cubes of paint in plastic containers. I often spent the evening with Grandfather Miller in his office, painting country scenes or creating ink and colour wash cartoons, our paints, brushes and jam jars full of water spread over his desktop. Grandfather was skilful at creating busy and humorous cartoons in a style reminiscent of those involving the wartime army characters, 'The Two Types' by Jon and the Giles family in the *Daily Express*. In my mid-teens David 'Beano' Green, a school friend from Repps, and I swapped meticulously produced pencil drawings of military aircraft, every detail checked for accuracy by reference to various aircraft magazines and books. Despite dropping Art as a subject after the third form at grammar school (to be replaced by Latin as, in the 1950s, Latin was still considered essential for any boy destined for university), I still managed to win the sixth form Art prize. This, however, was held in no great esteem among my peers, as it was considered by most masters and boys to be an award for a practical skill rather than for any intellectual achievement. I was not alone in my love of drawing and painting. My Birmingham cousin, Michael Cole, spent most of his holiday time at Great Yarmouth out and about painting local seaside and Broadland views. Cousin Pat Cole's future husband, John Clifford, a sign writer by trade, became well known as an accomplished local amateur artist and was an active member of the Yarmouth Guild of Artists and Craftsmen.

At university I found little time for painting and drawing; instead I was

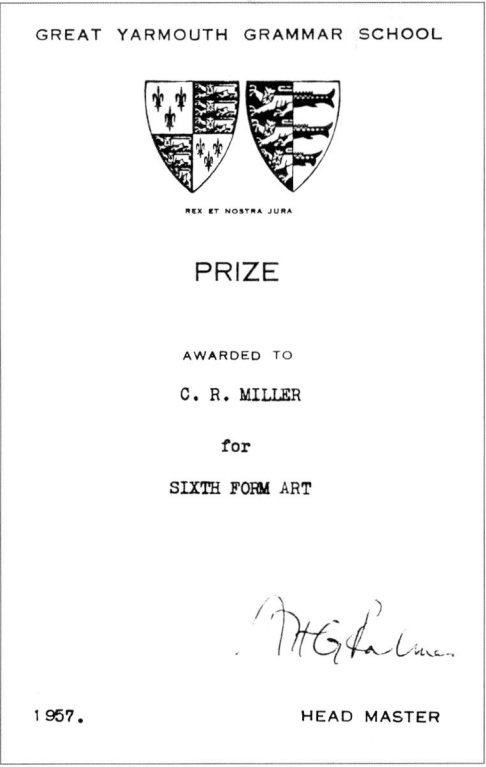

GREAT YARMOUTH GRAMMAR SCHOOL

REX ET NOSTRA JURA

PRIZE

AWARDED TO

C. R. MILLER

for

SIXTH FORM ART

1957.   HEAD MASTER

encouraged by my student friends to look at and appreciate art in all its forms. I discovered for the first time a world of paintings and sculpture in the museums and galleries of Norwich and Leicester. The walls of my room became covered in postcards depicting my favourite works of art, mainly paintings by Salvador Dali and Picasso. I gained quite a reputation for this collection and, on occasions, it became my alternative to etchings in initiating deep and meaningful conversations with female students. Once, when undoubtedly over-exaggerating my own artistic talents, my girlfriend of the time volunteered there and then to sit for me as a nude life model. In a moment of extreme naivety bordering on madness, I declined on the grounds that I had neither paints nor paper readily to hand. This offer was never repeated and our relationship soon ended.

I greatly enjoyed making models, initially as a ten-year-old with a second-hand set of Meccano pieces that was bought for me by my father. A small booklet provided instructions for making various machines, and together my father and I made models of cranes, lorries and aeroplanes. Often our constructions had to be abandoned when we discovered that the set was missing vital pieces. With my friend Richard, I used rubber moulds to make Plaster of Paris models of animals and Disney characters, which we painted, glazed and gave away to our family and friends. I also constructed a model of a yacht with a collapsible mast and sails held in place by string rigging, which I sailed on the Town Pit and at a small boating lake on the seafront in Gorleston. My interest in model making was further stimulated when, one Christmas, Uncle George Miller gave me a Frog construction kit for making a model aeroplane. The resulting model, powered by a propeller turned by a tightly wound elastic band, provided many hours of entertainment before eventually disintegrating on impact with a brick wall. Nevertheless, Richard and I enthusiastically tackled more and more complicated construction kits in an out-building at his father's farm, which we had turned into a workshop. We spent hours pressing out pieces from sheets of balsa wood and gluing them together with modeller's cement to form the framework of an

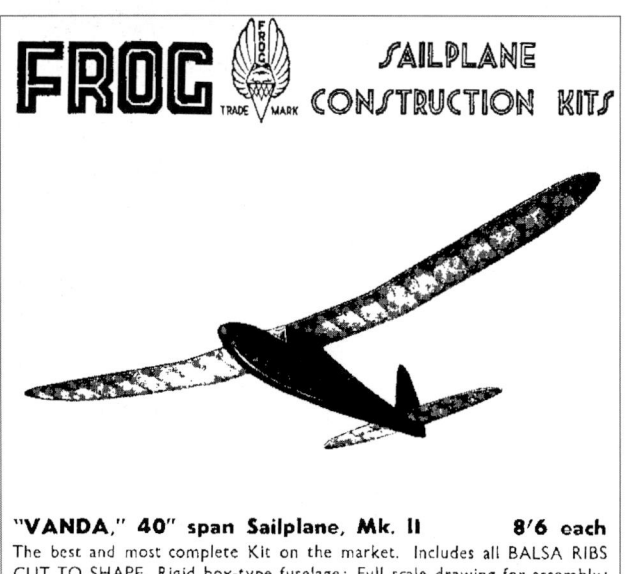

FROG TRADE MARK **SAILPLANE CONSTRUCTION KITS**

"VANDA," 40" span Sailplane, Mk. II   8/6 each

The best and most complete Kit on the market. Includes all BALSA RIBS CUT TO SHAPE. Rigid box-type fuselage; Full scale drawing for assembly; TISSUE; CLEAR DOPE; COLOURED DOPE; PASTE; CEMENT; CLEAR CABIN COVER and INSIGNIA. A really complete Kit with an amazing performance. There are no extras to buy.

aeroplane or ship. The completed framework was then covered with a paper-thin fabric, hardened with a proofing agent and painted. Finished models adorned both of our bedrooms or hung on thread from the rafters of the workshop. Any attempt to fly our models normally met with disaster, as they were simply meant for display.

However, undaunted, Richard once managed to acquire a miniature rocket engine which we attached to one of the models by string. A cylindrical block of fuel was placed inside the engine and ignited by a short fuse lit by a match. From behind the door of the workshop we watched open mouthed as the rocket-powered model failed to take to the air but careered drunkenly around the farmyard, bouncing off walls and other obstacles until, in less than a minute, there was little left of either model or engine.

LEISURE TIME FOR THE FAMILY

'Garden of Eden', Frankie Vaughan, 1957

While my parents had no real hobbies, they filled their spare time at home in the evenings and at weekends with activities that they not only enjoyed, but which also provided a useful end product. Despite the fact that she had to cook a main meal most days, mother loved baking and spent at least one evening every week making cakes, buns and tarts for pleasure as well as for our consumption. After clearing away the teatime meal, the dining table was covered with bags of flour, cubes of butter and margarine, eggs, milk, dried fruit, jam and her well-used bottle of vanilla essence. Various combinations of these ingredients were mixed in a large light-brown bowl. Dough was kneaded, rolled out on a flour-covered board and stamped into circles by tin cutters. The raw results were placed or poured into tins of various shapes and sizes, or into a dozen or more circular depressions in a rectangular pan, then placed in the oven to bake. While the smell of baking cakes permeated the air, we were offered the dubious privilege of 'scraping out the bowl', an honour my father greatly enjoyed. For myself, I could never understand the attraction of eating uncooked gunge adhering to the side of a mixing bowl. Eventually, baking was finished and mother's mixtures had been transformed, depending on what was being made, into rectangular slabs of currant-filled Norfolk shortcake, yellow saffron buns, large tins of gooey almond tart which she cut into tea-plate sized pieces, deliciously soft date slices, round custard tarts dusted with nutmeg, toffee-like jam tarts which she always over-baked, macaroons, syrup and coconut buns or dark-brown ginger cakes which became much stickier when left to age. The two halves of a sponge cake were stuck together with homemade jam and showered with icing sugar, and large brown fruitcakes were parted carefully from the greaseproof linings of their baking tins. My father and I could hardly wait to sample her produce and a dozen or more warm buns or slices of cake frequently disappeared with our suppertime cups of tea.

Typical of many men during the 1950s, my father and I had little interest in cooking – we were more interested in eating food than preparing it. Whenever mother was unavailable to cook our dinner we ate take-away meals from the fish and chip shop in Martham. On those few occasions when my father had to cook his speciality was boiled onions, which he ate smothered in pepper and salt. My repertoire consisted solely of porridge and custard. My lack of culinary skills proved to be a real problem when I eventually became a flat dweller in Leicester. However, not all men in the 1950s were similarly inclined. As his leisure time hobby, Uncle Frank Hammond derived both pleasure and relaxation from developing his personal skills as a baker and confectioner. For one of my birthdays, he made for me a birthday cake iced to look like a wicker basket with a bird's nest under its lid.

Mother was also good at handicrafts, especially knitting. Most of my jumpers and pullovers were home produced, often decorated with cable stitch and occasionally multi-coloured in a Fair Isle style, but mostly grey. In winter, she knitted balaclava helmets on bendy knitting pins for me to wear on the way to school, for summer she knitted my cricket sweaters with a black and red trim, the colours of Great Yarmouth Grammar School. Knitting wool was readily available, not only from Yarmouth's department stores, but also from most drapers and from Olivette's, a specialist wool shop in Market Row. On many evenings, either my father or I sat with our arms held out in front of us holding skeins of wool for mother to wind into balls. While she was knitting, she always placed the working ball inside a red beehive-shaped plastic container to prevent interruptions from our playful cats. Her collection of knitting pins was wrapped in a large brown paper bag and stored in the sideboard together with a pile of knitting patterns. As well as clothes for the family, she also knitted cushion covers, tea cosies, covers for our hot-water bottles and for the sausage-shaped draught excluders that were placed along the bottom of our living room doors. She even taught me to knit and I became quite adept at plain and pearl stitch but could never properly cast off. At the age of seven I was able to knit long multi-coloured scarves for my bedtime companions from odd pieces of leftover wool. She was of the opinion that men should be taught to knit, pointing out that the award for best knitter at Rollesby's summer fête was often won by Mr Hun, a retired lighthouse keeper. In the late 1940s and early '50s, mother's handicraft skills were certainly useful in the austere times immediately after the war. Our fireside rag mats were made from strips of material that she wove on to a Hessian backing, and our clothes were altered and repaired on an ancient black and gold Singer sewing machine. Many of her everyday clothes were homemade using bought patterns, each pattern consisting of numerous tissue paper shapes that she pinned onto lengths of material and cut round with a large pair of scissors. Once sewn together, the pieces made up a skirt, blouse, apron or dress, usually in a gaudy floral design. Her attempts to make shirts for my father were less successful. Evening dressmaking classes and knitting circles were a common occurrence and well attended during the 1950s.

ARTS & CRAFTS EXHIBITION

A display of work done during the year in arts and crafts was held in the County Primary School, which was open to parents, who saw examples of woodwork and woven articles such as scarves, cushion covers and pullovers. The standard of the needlework, embroidery and knitting was high.

'Village news, Martham', *Yarmouth Mercury*, 31 March 1950

Civil Defence training, 1955. Mother and grandmother (extreme right) optimistically learning how to make a field kitchen from the rubble left after a nuclear explosion. (Author's Collection)

Like many women during the 1950s, my mother and Grandmother Miller devoted a great deal of their spare time to community-based voluntary work. Together they organised village collections for various flag days, including the annual British Legion Poppy Day Appeal and whist drives on behalf of blind ex-servicemen, and both of them were members of the Women's Voluntary Service (WVS) and the local Civil Defence Corps. Through the WVS they helped to organise the distribution of clothing among needy villagers and attended courses of instruction in the care and needs of the elderly. Their civil defence training included day and evening courses on

CIVIL DEFENCE
CORPS
WELFARE

emergency feeding and care of the injured, should the need arise from a nuclear war with Russia. I read with great interest and some foreboding her instruction pamphlets on how to cope with the after effects of an atomic explosion. Had such a war occurred, it was clear even then that their efforts would be useless. However, the Civil Defence Corps training proved extremely useful during the east coast floods of 1953.

Although as a bricklayer he had no equal, my father's craft skills were limited. Nevertheless, undaunted, he embarked on numerous creative enterprises that resulted in products only he thought were eminently saleable. In a rented ex-wartime Nissen hut at Rollesby Hall, he made fireplace surrounds, eventually graduating to birdbaths and garden ornaments. From wire netting bent to shape, then covered in a concrete mix and gloss painted, he produced ornamental swans for sale at 10s each. I have no recollection of anyone buying one of his swans, only of numerous unsold misshapen concrete birds gracing our flower borders. He even unsuccessfully started producing toffee apples for Uncle Robert Cole to sell at his café in Gorleston. Other than laying bricks, his skills were confined to gardening, an activity he enjoyed immensely. During the summer our large garden supplied mother with a succession of vegetables, salad and fruit. Not only did our meals include freshly grown produce, but mother was also able to provide for the leaner winter months by storing apples in our spare bedroom, bottling fruit in Kilner jars and making jams, pickled onions and chutneys. My father's real passion, however, was for growing tomatoes and cucumbers in his homemade greenhouses and frames. His garden sheds, greenhouses and cucumber frames were created in a Heath Robinson manner from old windows, doors and reclaimed bricks salvaged from his building sites. Every morning and evening he watered his tomato plants, nipped out unwanted buds and tied the growing stems to canes. At the peak of production, his surplus produce was sold to neighbours and any passers-by that he engaged in conversation. Often, my tea consisted entirely of bread and butter with a plate full of freshly picked tomatoes soaked in vinegar and covered in salt. The cucumbers always gave me indigestion despite my father's assertion that the variety he had grown was called 'burpless' and was guaranteed not to upset a delicate stomach. When Grandfather Miller finally retired in the mid-1950s, he took over the running of grandfather's small market garden at the Field and continued to produce flowers, fruit and vegetables, mostly for sale at Great Yarmouth's weekly markets. At the end of the 1950s he cleared the ground in order to produce French beans for Birds Eye to freeze at their Yarmouth-based factory.

Most village properties (the tied cottages and council houses as well as the residences of the better off) had large well-cultivated gardens, mostly devoted to producing food for the table. Front, as well as back gardens were often planted with vegetables and salad crops, rather than laid down to lawn and flowers. When I complained about the lack of lawn space in our garden, my father retorted that 'You can't eat grass.' At weekends and evenings during the summer months many of the village menfolk spent long hours tending their gardens, some even rented village allotments. Grandfather Miller maintained an immaculate cottage garden at his home in Hall Cottages, his flower, fruit and vegetable areas arranged geometrically with each area bordered by a 2ft-high evergreen box hedge. Owing to its unique location, built on a thin strip of land sandwiched between marshes and the sea, most householders in Great Yarmouth, including my Cole relatives, had little or no garden suitable for cultivation. To compensate, Yarmouth was surrounded by acre upon acre of allotments that were fully occupied by urban gardeners in the 1950s.

If my father had a hobby, then it was gambling, particularly betting on horses. Every day he studied the racing pages in the *Daily Express* intently, picking out potential winners, searching through the results of the previous day and recording the performances of selected horses in a small red notebook. At lunchtime on most Saturdays, he walked to the Horse & Groom car park where he was able to place a bet with a man in a car who toured around the villages on behalf of a local bookmaker, collecting dues and paying out any winnings from the previous week. Not that he risked much in his betting. His maximum stake per bet was never more than 6*d* or possibly 1*s* if he had money to spare. To maximise his potential returns he used combination bets called Yankees and Patents. A Yankee involved four horses in a combination bet of six doubles, four trebles and a four horse accumulator, eleven bets altogether; while a Patent, three horses in three singles, three doubles and one treble, seven bets in total. Mother and I were occasionally regaled with tales of impressive wins. The regular long periods of silence between these tales suggested that such wins were few and far between. Every week he also completed a coupon for Vernon's football pools, convinced that he would eventually become the winner of the £75,000 jackpot. His pools entry was completed in 'plans' involving various selections of eight teams from a longer list. He was even tempted to respond to a radio advert in which a Mr Horace Batchelor, of Keynsham near Bristol, claimed to have a foolproof system for winning the jackpot. Nevertheless, the system was very soon deemed to be 'a swiz' and abandoned. His addiction to bingo, an emergent craze in the early 1960s, was inevitable. He spent at least two evenings every week in various local village halls crossing off numbers on a card in an attempt to win a small money prize.

3

Reading, Listening & Watching

READING MATTER

'The Book', David Whitfield, 1954

My parents were not great readers or, to be accurate, not great readers of books. I have no memory of either of them ever reading a novel. I can remember a pile of six or more books beside the front room fireplace, but these included a Bible, an English dictionary, a medical handbook and three books on building techniques, and were for occasional reference. Nevertheless, my parents were regular readers of newspapers and magazines, as were most of my family. The *Daily Express* was delivered to our home on every weekday, on Friday, the *Great Yarmouth Mercury*, on Saturday evening, the *Pink 'un* sports paper, and on Sunday, the *Sunday Express* and the *Sunday Pictorial*. Occasionally my father would also buy a copy of the *Eastern Daily Press* on his way to work. These were all read thoroughly from front to back, from the headline news to the sports pages, even when daily newspapers gained extra pages as the effects of wartime receded and paper became more readily available. In my father's case, the sports pages were always read first. Grandma Cole, retired and a widow, spent most of her time at home alone sitting in her armchair by the fire reading the local newspaper, her National Health wire-rimmed spectacles perched on the end of her nose, a Craven A cork-tipped cigarette in her mouth and a bottle of Guinness by her side, the silence broken only by the ticking of the clock on the sideboard. Every entry in the births, marriages and deaths section was carefully scrutinised in case it involved someone she knew. Like my parents, I also read newspapers from an early age and, as a consequence, was quite well versed in current affairs and national sporting news, albeit derived from potentially biased viewpoints. At Yarmouth Grammar School, 'respectable' daily newspapers were displayed on lecterns in the main hall for the boys to read. As I recall, most newspapers of the 1950s were 'respectable'. Pin-up photographs were rare, sex and scandal only occasionally dominated the daily headlines and even Grandfather Miller's Sunday *News of the World* used innuendo to comment on people's misbehaviour.

Once I could read, my preferred leisure time reading material was comics, in particular the *Beano*, *Dandy*, *Radio Fun* and *Film Fun*. My favourite characters in the

Happy Holidays at Gt. Yarmouth Tommy Trinder

" You Lucky People ! "

Beano were Lord Snooty in his suit and top hat and the terrible Dennis the Menace in his red and black stripy jumper. I adored the ever-popular cow pie-eating Desperate Dan and the mischievous Keyhole Kate in the *Dandy*. I laughed at the amusing adventures of the well known stars Tommy Trinder, Ted Ray, Tommy Handley, Arthur Askey and Flanagan and Allen in *Radio Fun*, as well as those screen favourites of my childhood, Laurel and Hardy, Abbott and Costello and dear Old Mother Riley in *Film Fun*. I even learned French through reading Tintin comics. The storylines were simple and funny and, while there was slapstick, violence was mostly absent, much to my mother's approval. In a less throw-away society, comics were saved, perused again and again or swapped for unread editions. In one such exchange, I managed to acquire numerous pre-war copies of *The Hotspur*. In January 1951, I was a victim of that year's influenza epidemic and spent a month away from school. One of my convalescent treats was a parcel of comics sent to me by my mother's London friend, Sally Pitchford, whom she had first met when Sally and her son, Peter, were wartime evacuees in Rollesby. Most of these were American comics, very popular at that time with teenage boys, but not the type of comic that I was used to. Their content was more akin to storybooks in pictures than children's comics – westerns, detective stories and adventures involving various superhuman characters that were capable of amazing and realistically impossible feats. Violent episodes were frequent and drawn in graphic detail, accompanied by various new additions to the English language, words such as 'Splaaat', 'Aaaaaaargh', 'Biff', 'Kerraashh' and the like.

Mother much preferred me to read the *Eagle* comic, a colourful, entertaining and educational magazine for boys created in 1950 by the Revd Marcus Morris as a reaction to the influx of these violent and occasionally horrific American comic books, a magazine in which the heroes were realistically human and right always prevailed over wrong. Like many other boys, I became addicted to the *Eagle* and proudly wore my gold Eagle Club members badge on my jacket lapel. I even bought an Eagle Club diary. Every week, I followed with interest the exploits of Daniel McGregor Dare, pilot of the future, his batman, Digby, and their conflicts on Venus with the gruesome green Mekon. I might even have noticed and registered the unusual fact that Dan's intellectual friend, Professor Peabody, was a woman. Not only did I follow with interest the adventures of PC49, Harris Tweed and Luck of the Legion, but I was also educated and informed by the scientific explanations of Professor Britain, the true-life biographies of famous sports personalities and British heroes, the useful sports coaching and the innovative centrefold cutaway pictures of buildings and machines that I studied in minute detail. In 1952, I also subscribed to the *Lion* with its Dan Dare-like hero, Captain Condor, but no other comic had the same appeal for me as the *Eagle*.

By the time I was sixteen comics had lost their attraction, even the *Eagle*. Comics were replaced by subscriptions to *Flight International* and, from 1956, the newly-established *New Scientist*. Not that I understood all of their content, my interest being mainly in items about military aircraft and astronomy, but they seemed appropriate for a student preparing to study mathematics and science at A-level. Like most adolescent boys of the time, I also scoured carefully through editions of

National Geographic in the school library, learning much about foreign lands and peoples, and sniggering at pictures of bare-breasted native women. In the sixth form common room we read back numbers of *Punch*. Mother had a regular order for two women's magazines, the *Woman* and *Woman's Own*. Occasionally she also bought editions of *Woman's Realm* in a search of cooking recipes and knitting patterns. In addition to their newspapers, my Miller grandparents read two popular current affairs magazines, the *Illustrated* and the *Picture Post*, which they passed on to us when they had finished with them.

Woman's Own special souvenir issue, 1960.

As most parents read to their younger children every night, I presume that mother read to me. She said that I was particularly fond of *Gulliver's Travels*, which she first read to me at the age of five when I was ill with measles – not an obvious choice for a young boy. However, once I could read for myself, my preferred reading was non-fiction and my most treasured books during the 1940s were a picture book on trains, a wartime aircraft recognition manual, a nature book on animals of the world, another about British birds and a world atlas. I spent many happy hours looking at the maps in the atlas, learning about the oceans and countries around the world, and memorising the names of the cities, rivers and mountains. By the time I went to grammar school, I had not read many children's classics. Those that I owned were given to me as Christmas presents and included *Treasure Island*, *Lorna Doone*, *Kidnapped*, *David Copperfield* and *Black Beauty*, the last two undoubtedly because of their association with Great Yarmouth. Those that I liked I read again and again, particularly *Treasure Island* and *Lorna Doone*. I frequently imagined myself as a brave and gallant hero in pursuit of an attractive Lorna Doone, but in character I preferred to be more like Carver Doone than John Ridd. At grammar school, I was encouraged to read more and in order to help me I was registered as a reader at the Public Library in Great Yarmouth. Unfortunately for my education, I preferred borrowing westerns to literary classics. I also borrowed books from my friend Richard, especially his storybooks about *Just William*, the *Famous Five* and the *Secret Seven*.

In my later teens, I still preferred non-fiction and this was a great disappointment to my English teacher, Mr Pashley. English literature was one of my failures at school. The only time I showed any enthusiasm for the subject was when my class was introduced to the Hornblower novels, which struck an immediate chord, as I was by then a fanatical admirer of Lord Nelson, another Norfolk boy. Generally, I found the language of Shakespeare unintelligible and the storylines of Dickens too complicated. Any knowledge I had of classical literature was gained primarily from the cinema, the radio and, eventually, television, not from books. However, I did read again and again a book given to me by my Grandfather Miller – an 1897 leather-bound edition of *The Talisman*, part of the Waverley Novels by Sir Walter Scott, which he had been awarded as a prize when a schoolboy at the Priory Upper Grade School in Great Yarmouth. For leisure reading I mainly enjoyed the adventures of Biggles by Captain W.E. Johns, and paperback books about military exploits in the Korean and Second World Wars, particularly those of the Desert Rats and the Glorious Gloucesters. Beside my bed at home, I had a collection of I-Spy books written by Big Chief I-Spy, Charles Warrell, which encouraged young people to look about them and to learn from what they could see and do. During our sixth form years, Tim and I discovered the delights of Mr Ferrow's, a second-hand bookshop on Howard Street between Market Row and Broad Row, a district of Great Yarmouth that allegedly contained numerous illegal drinking dens and houses of ill repute much loved by visiting off-duty American servicemen. Tim and I scoured the dusty interior of Mr Ferrow's on most Saturdays, searching through the piles of books that lay scattered over the floors and shelves of his shop for cheap paperback novels and useful reference books on mathematics and science.

Mr Ferrow, a short stocky middle-aged man with sharp eyes, monitored our progress from behind his desk in the back room. Once aware of our interests, he could always locate a relevant book from among the apparent chaos around him.

At university, my reading was mostly related to the modules in my degree course, an interesting combination of mathematics, the history and philosophy of science and British archaeology. I found little time for leisure reading but what I did read – on average about one book a month, non-fiction as well as fiction – was greatly influenced by my student friends and was mostly literature which dealt with social issues of the time. Typically, these were the contemporary and popular 'kitchen sink' novels that explored the existing class divisions in British society and the problems associated with being working class, an issue I clearly identified with. Written by the so-called 'angry young men', these included Alan Sillitoe's *Saturday Night and Sunday Morning* and *The Loneliness of the Long Distance Runner*, and John Braine's *Room at the Top*, although in many cases I actually saw the film of the book first. I even tried to read James Joyce's *Ulysses*, but failed completely to comprehend any of its content, even the risqué bits. In 1960, once the obscenity trial was over and it became generally available in bookshops, I was bought a Penguin edition of D.H. Lawrence's infamous novel *Lady Chatterley's Lover* by my then girlfriend. Every evening she rang me on a public telephone to enquire how much I had read. Despite her obvious fascination with the book, I could never persuade her to act out any of the more interesting episodes of the storyline. However, my best remembered readings from that period are not popular bestsellers but three lesser known works – the astronomer Fred Hoyle's thought-provoking science-fiction novel *The Black Cloud* and Geoffrey Household's suspense stories *Rogue Male* and *The Watcher in the Shadows*.

LISTENING TO THE RADIO

'Bluebottle blues', The Goons, 1956

Before the advent of television, newspapers and the radio were our main sources of news, information and entertainment. In our Rollesby home, we had neither a television nor a record player until the late 1950s. Our radio, a large brown Bakelite set, sat on a small table on the far side of the living room. There it remained, as most radios were not portable and needed a permanent electrical connection. Our radio also needed an aerial as the reception on Norfolk's east coast was often variable and prone to interference from continental stations. The aerial consisted of a long wire that wound its way from the back of the radio along the skirting board, through the pantry window and up the side of the house. Mother turned the radio on every morning as soon as she got up and, as long as somebody was at home, it remained on until my father turned it off last thing at night. During the day it was a background accompaniment while mother did her housework, in the evening it provided all the family with varied entertainments to relax to. Most daytime programmes were of popular music, undoubtedly intentionally designed so as to provide a pleasant environment as people went about their daily business. From Monday to Friday, many of Yarmouth's factories played radio music through speakers to their workers, a habit acquired during the war as a means of encouraging maximum production. I frequently passed Grouts' textile factory on St Nicholas Road in Great Yarmouth on my way to visit one of my aunts, pausing on occasions to peer through an open door at the activity inside, my ears assailed by the clanking of the machinery, the sound of loud music from the radio and the often off-key singing of the workers.

At Rollesby, my parents and I normally listened to the BBC Home Service, the Light programme, and, if the reception permitted, Radio Luxembourg – the Home

SUNDAY 8 OCTOBER 1950

9.30	*Music in the Air*	4.45	Sam Costa's *Record Rendezvous*
10.30	Wilfred Pickles in *Have a Go*	6.00	*Round Britain Quiz*
12.00	Joe Loss and His Orchestra	7.30	*Grand Hotel*
12.30	*Family Favourites*	9.00	*Variety Bandbox*
2.30	Richard Dimbleby in *Down Your Way*	10.15	Ivor Moreton & Dave Kaye on two pianos
3.30	Peter Brough in *Educating Archie*	10.45	Sandy MacPherson on the theatre organ

SUNDAY 9 OCTOBER 1955

10.00	*Silver Chords in the Air*	5.30	Victor Silvester and His Orchestra
11.00	Wilfred Pickles in *Have a Go*	6.30	*Journey into Space*
12.00	*Two-Way Family Favourites*	7.00	*The Frankie Howerd Show*
1.45	Peter Brough in *Educating Archie*	8.15	Semprini and His Orchestra
2.15	*British Bandbox*	10.15	*Grand Hotel*
3.30	*Melody Hour*	10.30	*Down Melody Lane*

SUNDAY 9 OCTOBER 1960

9.45	*The Archers* Omnibus Edition	2.45	*Movie-go-round*
10.30	*Easy Beat*	5.00	Richard Dimbleby in *Down Your Way*
12.00	*Two-Way Family Favourites*	6.00	*Sing Something Simple*
1.15	*The Billy Cotton Band Show*	7.35	*Just for You*
1.45	*Meet the Huggetts*	9.00	*Follow the Stars*
2.15	Ted Ray in *Ray's a Laugh*	10.40	Pete Murray

Sundays on the BBC Light Programme, 1950–60.

Service for news, drama and big band music, the Light for popular music, situation comedy and variety shows. We hardly ever listened to the Third programme, as we considered its content to be too 'posh' for our tastes. I was particularly fond of Radio Luxembourg because its programmes were teenage-orientated and consisted mainly of current popular music, a fondness not shared by my parents. In self-defence, my father bought a radio for my bedroom, a large modern-looking brown and cream set with a row of six press-buttons for pre-selected stations. Thereafter, I spent many evenings either on my bed or staring out of my bedroom window listening to my favourite programmes.

During my student days at Leicester, access to a radio was limited. Not that this mattered much as, in my leisure time, I preferred to talk with student friends, strum a guitar, play at cards or listen to records. In Leicester University's Beaumont Hall of Residence, nobody that I knew owned a personal radio. The only access to radio programmes was via a rarely used radiogram located in a small back room of the main building. Most of the flats where I lived subsequently had a radio in their communal sitting rooms, big old-fashioned sets with large speakers and valve-illuminated interiors. These were used only occasionally, mainly for listening to Radio Luxembourg, jazz or popular music programmes. It was not until 1963 that I finally spent £8 at Stone's Lighting & Radio Ltd in the centre of Leicester on the latest technological craze – a small blue and silver battery-powered transistor radio with an extendible aerial. This was a neat and eminently portable set that not only provided non-stop entertainment at home but also enlivened walks in the park and long train journeys back to Norfolk, much to the annoyance of my fellow travellers.

By the 1950s I had progressed beyond children's radio, *Uncle Mac* and *Toytown*, preferring comedy programmes and, eventually, popular music. The earliest situation comedy I can recall was *ITMA* (It's That Man Again) with Tommy Handley, a series that provided much needed mirth on the radio during the dark days of the Second World War and after. Not that I remember now, or even understood then, the comedic situations that it described. I remember it for the characters involved and their catchphrases – Jack Train as Colonel Chinstrap, the inebriated army officer who turned every conversation into an offer of a drink; 'I don't mind if I do', and Dorothy Summers as the cleaner, Mrs Mopp, announcing her presence with 'Can I do you now Sir'. Like most of the nation, my parents were very upset when Tommy Handley died suddenly in 1949 and this long running series ended. In the 1950s, I laughed at the adventures of Richard Murdoch and Kenneth Horne at the RAF station in Much-binding-in-the-Marsh; Jimmy Edwards, June Whitfield and Dick Bentley as the Glum family in *Take it from Here* ('Oh Ron', 'Yes Eth'), and Tony Hancock in *Hancock's Half Hour* with Kenneth Williams' regular request for Hancock to 'Stop messing about'. *Bedtime with Braden*, *Meet the Huggetts*, *Educating Archie* and *Beyond Our Ken*, to name but a few, made listening to the radio a great pleasure and gave opportunities for listeners to use their imaginations in a way not possible while watching a television show. In common with most teenagers of the 1950s, my absolute favourite comedy series was *The Goon Show*, a zany programme with unreal idiotic characters invented by Peter Sellers, Harry Secombe, Spike Milligan and Michael Bentine. The programme's mad alternative humour certainly struck a chord and my friends and I undoubtedly infuriated many of our older generation, including my parents and most of the masters at Yarmouth Grammar School, with our imitations of *The Goon Show* characters: Neddy Seagoon, Major Bloodnok, Minnie Bannister, Bluebottle and Eccles, and a few frequently repeated phrases such as 'You rotten swine, you've deaded me' and 'He's fallen in the water.'

On my bedroom radio I listened intently to the adventures of Jet Morgan, Lemmy and Doc in *Journey into Space* on the Light Programme, and also those of the *Eagle* comic's Dan Dare in a radio series sponsored by Horlicks on Radio Luxembourg, the Station of the Stars, at 208 on Medium Wave. In the late 1950s, Radio Luxembourg became my preferred listening, especially at 11 p.m. on a Sunday evening when the latest Top 20 pop music charts were released. I listened avidly to this American-style commercial station while completing my homework, or when just simply passing time. I shouted answers at the radio during editions of *Take Your Pick* and *Double Your Money*, on Irish night I sang

'If you're Irish come into the Parlour', I memorised the commercial jingles and stamped my feet to non-stop pop music. Late at night I listened with my ear pressed hard against the speaker in case my father should hear and demand that I turn the radio off.

My parents preferred listening to dance band music, commentaries on any sporting event, particularly horse racing and football, and popular magazine programmes. During the day mother always found time for *Woman's Hour* and *Mrs Dale's Diary*, and, on Saturday night, we all listened to the interviews with contemporary celebrities and other 'odd' individuals appearing on *In Town Tonight*, a series that was always introduced by the announcement 'We stop the mighty roar of London's traffic and from the great crowds we bring you some of the interesting people who have come by land, sea and air to be in town tonight.' They rarely missed the weekly editions of Wilfred Pickles in *Have a Go* or Richard Dimbleby coming *Down Your Way*, especially when either programme was broadcast from a part of East Anglia. I was taught modern ballroom dance steps in our living room while listening to music played by Henry Hall, Victor Sylvester, Joe Loss or Edmundo Ross and their orchestras. Eventually, listening to the radio became a daytime occupation when the inevitable television set arrived.

WATCHING TELEVISION

'It's only make-believe', Conway Twitty, 1958

Despite most people's assertion that they acquired a television set for the Coronation of Queen Elizabeth II in 1953, television reception in our part of Norfolk was barely possible until the erection of the Tacolneston transmitter in 1956. Until then, I had seen a television set only once before on a visit to my Uncle George Miller's house in Bexley Heath, Kent, for Christmas 1950. His television, housed in a large dark-brown wooden cabinet, had a 10in green screen that, when turned on, produced a small black and white moving picture. That holiday, we spent the evenings of Christmas Eve and Christmas Day in a semi-circle in front of this cabinet staring hard at the faint flickering images on the screen before us instead of playing the usual party games, much to the disappointment of a ten-year-old me. When Tacolneston came on line in 1956, Uncle Cecil Miller at Rollesby post office became the first locally based member of our family to buy his own set. Every Sunday, mother, father and I, and occasionally my grandparents, were invited for tea and to watch the early evening programmes. I usually arrived by 4.30 p.m. as the children's teatime programmes on most Sundays were short cowboy films featuring at various times Hopalong Cassidy, the Range Rider, the Cisco Kid and the Lone Ranger with his faithful Indian companion, Tonto. In 1956, a convenient interval still existed between the children's and adult programmes, allowing tea to be taken at the table while the television displayed either a test card, a seemingly never-ending image of a potter at his wheel or a kitten playing with a ball of wool. The notion of television meals taken on knees while continuing to watch the screen was still unacceptable in our family. After tea, we all watched television again from 7 p.m. until the end of *What's My Line*, when we went home.

When Tacolneston became fully operational in 1957, my parents bought their first television set from Wolsey & Wolsey of Great Yarmouth, a Bush television with a 14in screen that cost my father almost £50. Placed firmly on its own wheeled stand, the new television took pride of place against the wall on the far side of our living room. In order to receive the programmes, a large H-shaped aerial was fixed on top of a long metal pole erected in the garden because the chimney was considered too weak to support it. The black and white pictures were not always clear as the reception was often variable and susceptible to interference caused by adverse atmospheric conditions, passing traffic or electronic machinery, particularly the milking machines of Hall Farm opposite our house on Martham Road. My father mistakenly considered himself to be an expert in all things electronic and spent many hours fiddling with the control knobs at the front and back of the set in a valiant attempt to improve the picture. The contrast, brilliance, vertical and horizontal hold controls were all adjusted with little effect save, on occasions, when the picture appeared to exist in a snow storm, roll up and down, or come away from the side of the screen in a zigzag pattern.

Initially, it was only possible to receive a single channel broadcast by the BBC and, consequently, there was no choice of programme. However, my parents were hooked and watching television became their main form of entertainment in the evenings and at weekends. Whist drives, dances and other social activities became a thing of the past. In the autumn of 1959, Anglia Television – a commercial channel for the East of England – was launched and choice became an issue and, inevitably, the cause of many arguments. Not only my parents but also some of my friends became addicted to television. Our living room was regularly occupied by many of my square-eyed friends until their parents too became television owners. Apart from some notable exceptions, I found the majority of programmes tedious and boring, and less appealing than playing sport, meeting friends or chasing females. As a result, television made little impact on my teenage lifestyle in the late 1950s, but for my parents and many of my contemporaries it constituted a major force for change.

Nevertheless, a few programmes did have a special appeal. These were mainly sports programmes including midweek editions of *Sportsview*, weekend *Sports Special* and, eventually, *Grandstand*. Their presenters, Peter Dimmock, Kenneth Wolstenholme and David Coleman, were quite influential in introducing me to and developing my knowledge and understanding of many new and different sporting activities. I saw my first rugby match on television. Another programme that had a great influence on my life was *Animal, Vegetable, Mineral?*, a quiz programme presented by Glyn Daniel in which eminent archaeologists, including Mortimer Wheeler, Gordon Childe and Jacquetta Hawkes, were challenged to identify objects taken from the archaeological collections of different British museums. Mortimer Wheeler, an eccentric but brilliant man with long wavy hair and a bushy moustache, so inspired me with his television performances that he was the reason why I chose to study British archaeology as one element in my degree course at Leicester.

SATURDAY 5 DECEMBER 1959

BBC		Anglia TV	
1.00	*Grandstand*	1.15	*Lets Go Round of Sport*
5.00	*The Lone Ranger*	5.00	*Robin Hood*
5.25	*The Golden Nobles*	5.30	*Commentary Box*: local sport
6.00	*Laramie*	6.00	*The Invisible Man*
6.50	*Juke Box Jury*	6.30	Marty Wilde in *Boy Meets Girl*
7.15	*Dixon of Dock Green*	7.00	*Wyatt Earp*
8.35	*Saturday Playhouse*	7.28	*Epilogue to Capricorn*
10.05	*Sports Special*	8.00	Arthur Askey in *Saturday Spectacular*
10.35	*Small World*	9.00	*Four Just Men*
11.05	*Max Jaffa*	9.30	*Great Movies of our Time*

SUNDAY 6 DECEMBER 1959

BBC		Anglia TV	
12.40	*Farming*	11.15	*Church Service*
2.00	*Ask Me Another*	1.15	*American Ten-pin Bowling*
2.25	Film: *It's a Wonderful Life*	2.30	*Farming Diary*
5.05	*The Young Lady from London*	3.10	*Film Festival*
5.40	*Snap Shot*	4.55	*Carroll Levis' Junior Discoveries*
7.00	*Meeting Point*	5.20	*William Tell*
7.30	*Showtime* with David Nixon	7.30	*Interpol Calling*
8.15	*What's My Line?*	8.00	*Sunday Night at the London Palladium*
8.45	*Sunday Night Theatre*	9.05	*Armchair Theatre*
10.05	*Monitor*	10.05	*Cheyenne*

Selected programmes from a weekend's television viewing.

Other than these, my interest was solely in popular music programmes, particularly the innovative *6.5 Special*, so named because it started at five past six on a Saturday evening. Produced by Jack Good for the BBC and presented by Pete Murray, Josephine Douglas and the boxer, Freddie Mills, this programme popularised jazz, skiffle and rock 'n' roll music with a teenage audience during 1957 and '58. Every Saturday without fail I watched the live performances of many of my favourite artists and resident bands, including the trombone-playing Don Lang and his Frantic Five, Johnnie Dankworth with Cleo Lane, John Barry, Lord Rockingham's Eleven, Jim Dale, Lonnie Donegan, and Marty Wilde. I watched the guitar instruction given by Bert Weedon with interest, although my considered opinion was that he was rather 'square'; I even tolerated Petula Clark's singing. When Jack Good left to produce ITV's *Oh Boy*, *6.5 Special* was replaced by *Drumbeat* and, eventually, in 1959, *Juke Box Jury* with David Jacobs in the chair.

For most of my time at university, my life was virtually television free. In 1959, there were no television sets in evidence in Beaumont Hall or at the main university site. Not that this mattered as I was fully occupied with academic studies, learning how to look after myself away from my mother's tender care and exploring to excess the abundant temptations to be found in a student's leisure time environment. Television sets in flats were also a rarity as they were far too expensive for students on a grant. Only once was a television installed in any of the various flats and houses where I lived and then only for a very short time. The television, an old battered set well past its use-by date, had been acquired by one of the other resident students primarily to watch the controversial programme *That Was The Week That Was* (TW3) hosted by a young David Frost. Every week for the month or two that the set continued to work, a dozen or more students gathered in our smoke-filled lounge to drink coffee and guffaw at the often politically sensitive sketches that made up most of the programme's content. The television was hardly ever used for any other viewing as we had no licence and were in constant fear of being discovered by the detector vans that were allegedly touring around our neighbourhood. I did not own a personal television set until 1964 when, as newlyweds, my wife and I were given a second-hand black and white set by her parents. The set actually arrived on the same day that I was away in Norwich for my first job interview. On my return, I had to wait patiently until the end of an episode of *Dr Kildare* before I was allowed to tell my wife the good news of my appointment.

From the late 1950s, my parents spent most of their evenings watching television. Their viewing consisted mainly of sports programmes, comedy, variety and quiz shows. They never missed *The Billy Cotton Band Show* or *Hancock's Half Hour*, both of which had made the successful transition from radio to television. Not so for *Educating Archie* or *The Goon Show*, as Peter Brough was shown clearly to be an inexpert ventriloquist and the depiction of the Goon characters as puppets was disastrous. They were transfixed by *Come Dancing* and sang along happily with the now politically incorrect *Black and White Minstrel Show*. At weekends they watched the slick *Perry Como Show* on Saturday, and *Sunday Night at the London Palladium* on Anglia, compèred by an energetic Bruce Forsyth. Unlike me, they

also enjoyed the many imported American situation comedies such as *I Love Lucy* with the zany Lucille Ball and her husband Desi Arnaz, *The Jack Benny Show* and *Life with the Lyons*, although Phil Silvers as Sergeant Bilko has subsequently achieved cult status with many, including me. It is abundantly clear to me that my parents were not exceptional and that the arrival of television in the 1950s did cause a major change in the leisure time activities of most people.

4

Village Entertainment

VISITING THE PUBLIC HOUSE

'Pub with no beer', Slim Dusty, 1959

For those willing to participate, it was virtually impossible to be bored with village life during the 1950s. Limited access to public or private motor transport restricted the ability of many villagers, including myself, to use the abundant entertainment facilities of Great Yarmouth and Norwich on a regular basis. As a result, all the village communities of rural Fleggs provided varied and well-supported homegrown entertainment for their inhabitants through numerous clubs, societies and organisations. There was always something to see or do in Rollesby or

St George's Church, Rollesby. Much of the social life in the village was associated with farming and the church. (Sheila Allen)

The Kings Arms, Martham. Every village had an inn or public house, which acted as a social centre for the village residents. (© Eastern Daily Press 2007)

in one of its neighbouring villages on most evenings and at weekends, activities and events which were normally held in local community halls, church and club rooms, school buildings and public houses, or at the village recreation field. Occasionally, some of these took place in private houses when a suitable venue was unavailable. The most traditional of these venues was the local pub. Every village possessed at least one inn, tavern, hotel bar or public house for use by their residents. Once I had reached the age of eighteen, or on some occasions well before the age of eighteen, I travelled by cycle to meet with my friends in the King's Arms by the pond at Martham, the Bridge Hotel at Potter Heigham, the Royal Oak adjacent to the Great Ormesby village green, the King's Head at Hemsby or at the Fleggburgh King's Arms.

Rollesby was served by two public houses, both of which I eventually knew intimately despite my parents' disapproval. The west of the village was catered for by the Horse & Groom, a typical small country pub situated on a corner where the Fleggburgh to Martham Road crossed the Main Road, opposite to Rollesby post office and a mere 50 yards from my home. The east of the village had the Eels Foot

The Horse & Groom, Rollesby was a typical small country public house that provided entertainment on most evenings for the working men and women of the village.
(Sheila Allen)

Inn, a broad-side establishment a short distance from the Main Road just over Rollesby Bridge into Little Ormesby, whose location was indicated by a large illuminated notice board alongside the main road pointing towards a small lane and stating 'Eels Foot Inn, 100 yards'. Although they were very different establishments, both pubs were well patronised by the local inhabitants. A third public house, the Sportsman's Arms, once existed close to Rollesby Bridge but was closed in the late 1940s to become a private house.

The Horse & Groom, a rectangular brick building with a central wooden pillared entrance porch, was a tied house belonging to Lacon's Brewery of Great Yarmouth and, throughout the 1950s, it was managed by Mr William 'Buster' Curtis and his wife. From the porch, the front entrance opened into a poorly lit through passage that, in turn, gave access to the public bar on the left, and a small narrow lounge or smoke room on the right. The public bar was long and thin with a wooden counter along the inside wall from which Buster, a thick set, red-faced jovial man with a mop of grey curly hair, served draught beer from three hand-pumps, usually Lacon's bitter, best and mild. Tables and chairs lined the other sides of the bar while a dartboard with a rubber mat in front was pinned to the far wall.

My drink of choice at eighteen was normally a mixture of mild and bitter served in a handled mug, as the sweetness of the mild covered up the sharpness of the aptly named bitter beer, a taste I had not yet come to appreciate. Lined up on shelves behind the counter were bottles containing Light Ale, Nut Brown Ale, Audit Ale,

Oatmeal Stout, mixers and soft drinks. Meals were not served in the pub but, for a snack, drinkers could purchase a packet of locally produced Smith's potato crisps that included a blue twisted paper sachet containing salt. Smith's crisps were extremely popular despite the awful sickly smell that emanated from Smith's Caister Road factory in Great Yarmouth. As I remember, in 1958 a pint and a packet of crisps cost little more than 1*s*. The bar itself was very much a male preserve, a traditional meeting place where men met to drink, play games and discuss important issues of the day. On Sunday mornings at five minutes to twelve, my mother would shake her head in despair at the line of men walking to the Horse & Groom for the lunchtime session, 12 noon until 2 p.m., bemoaning the fate of their wives and mothers left at home preparing the Sunday lunch.

By some unwritten convention, women used the bar facilities only if they were accompanied by their husbands or partners, or they were in a group such as the ladies' darts team. Otherwise, and in many cases out of preference, they used the small cramped lounge. Traditionally, Saturday night was partners' night, when many women joined their husbands for an evening at their local. As I recall, women hardly ever entered a public house without an escort. A woman alone, particularly in urban public houses, was a tempting target for men drawing wrong conclusions. Some

William 'Buster' Curtis, landlord of the Horse & Groom public house, Rollesby. During the 1950s the pub was tied to Lacon's Brewery of Great Yarmouth and draught beer was the norm. (Sheila Allen)

public houses placed benches in their central passageways which were not only used by those waiting for service at the pub's off-license window but frequently also by elderly and widowed ladies seeking company and conversation while partaking of a stout or something stronger. The Horse & Groom had two small wooden benches outside its main entrance for customers to use on dry evenings. I remember clearly sitting on one of those benches with a cousin of a cousin, Christopher, quaffing a pint of mild and bitter, surveying the millions of stars that were clearly visible in a sky untainted by street lights, identifying the various constellations among them and wondering at man's apparent insignificance in such an immense universe.

Although the Horse & Groom was popular and well frequented, drunkenness and under-age drinking was rare, undoubtedly because of the regular surveillance made by the village policeman. Before the age of eighteen, it was always easier for me to obtain alcoholic drinks elsewhere, mainly in Great Yarmouth, where I was not so well known and my age was not in doubt. Once I turned eighteen, I was able not only to drink alcohol with my friends, particularly after weekend cricket and football matches, but also to make use of the many other facilities provided by the public house. With Tim, Vick Kemp and Bill Brugger, I played crib, dominoes and darts while drinking a pint of beer as slowly as possible, discussing and solving the ills of the world as only young people can. In one Hemsby pub we regularly played table skittles and shove halfpenny. The skittle board consisted of a square base with a pole attached to one corner. Nine skittle pegs were placed on top of the base in a diamond formation, and from the top of the pole hung a ball on a string. The aim of the game was to swing the ball around the pole so as to knock down the skittle pegs. Frequently, in the heat of competition, the ball was projected with such enthusiasm that it swung out beyond the playing area, occasionally smashing a pint glass belonging to a nearby spectator, often with dire consequences. When alone, I scanned the newspapers that were laid on the counter for customers to read. Late in the evening it was not unusual for customers to break into song, usually popular sing-a-long tunes with an occasional local folksong thrown in by some old 'Norfolk boy' or folksong enthusiast. Occasionally the Horse & Groom was visited by well-known entertainers from Yarmouth's summer variety shows, some of whom were coerced into giving the regulars an impromptu performance. George Formby, who owned a riverside property in Wroxham, was a regular visitor to many Broadland public houses, including the Horse & Groom, and was often persuaded to sing a song or two. In 1950, a darts club was formed and entered teams into the newly re-established Lacon's Brewery Darts League. For most of the Horse & Groom regulars, darts was their game of choice and even friendly games were hotly contested.

DARTS CLUB DINNER

The Horse & Groom Darts Club held its annual dinner at the Blue Anchor Hotel, Yarmouth on Saturday. The Chairman, Mr C. Miller, welcomed the club's president Mr S. Gaze after his illness and accident. The hon. secretary, Miss S. Curtis, and captain, Mr S. Lambert, thanked the members for their part in a successful season.

'Village News, Rollesby', *Yarmouth Mercury*, 4 June 1954

An open area to the front and one side of the Horse & Groom was used for a variety of purposes including a car and cycle park, a bus stop, the location for a red telephone box (an essential facility at a time when few people possessed a personal telephone) and as a convenient gathering place for teenagers to meet and pass away the time. Every Saturday evening a mobile fish and chip van arrived to sell instant take-away meals to drinkers and nearby villagers. A pathway led through the pub's kitchen garden via a gate in a wooden fence to a well-tended bowling green, the

An evening out in the early 1950s. Aunt Doris and Uncle Cecil Miller with friends enjoying a sherry, cigarettes and conversation. (Carrie Spencer)

Rollesby Bowls Club, 1950. Most of the Flegg villages had a bowling green and a thriving bowls club. (Richard Tacon)

The Bowling Green, Rollesby. Positioned behind the Horse & Groom public house, the bowling green was the location for many hotly contested games of bowls in rain as well as sunshine. (Sheila Allen)

home venue of the Rollesby Bowls Club. In the 1950s, most villages of the Fleggs boasted a bowling green and a thriving bowls club, usually associated with the village public house. While the darts club attracted mainly the ordinary working men and women of the village, the bowls club was patronised by every social class. The gentleman farmer, the agricultural labourer, the road sweeper, the shop keeper, the doctor and the vicar all rubbed shoulders on the bowling green. In 1949, the Horse & Groom Bowls Club was instrumental in establishing the Flegg Bowls League, which was amalgamated with the Yarmouth & District Bowls League soon afterwards in order to promote competitive bowls throughout Great Yarmouth and the Fleggs. Both my father and grandfather were keen bowls players and possessed their own sets of bowls; grandfather's contained in a heavily polished leather case, my father's in a string bag. Grandmother Miller played competitive ladies' bowls on the seafront greens of Great Yarmouth. Every year an open bowls competition was held at the Horse & Groom for a silver Rose Bowl presented to the club by its President, Mr H. Marsden-Smith, a millionaire factory owner from Great Yarmouth who lived in the village. In 1956, my father returned home, a large grin on his face and the Marsden-Smith Rose Bowl under his arm, declaring in his usual unassuming manner, 'I won.' The Rose Bowl sat for the next year on the living room sideboard without any thought given to the fact that it might be worth money and a suitable target for a thief. I played bowls as a teenager but not with any great enthusiasm – more in the hope of being bought a half of bitter by one of my older playing partners.

The Eels Foot Inn in Little Ormesby was a brick-built, double bay-fronted building also serving Lacon's ales and set in an idyllic location at the end of a short lane beside the shore of Ormesby Broad. Its position attracted not only local drinkers but also fishermen and sightseers, and was a regular destination for summer coach parties from nearby Great Yarmouth and the Caister Holiday Camp. The public bar was typical of many Broad-side inns with the walls covered in old local photographs, fishing tackle and display cases containing the stuffed remains of immense pike that had been caught in the waters of Trinity Broad. From the shoreline in front of the inn rowing boats, moored against an L-shaped jetty, were available for hire by fishing parties, holidaymakers and young couples seeking privacy among the reeds. Between the inn and the jetty, a large wooden boatshed had been converted into a refreshment room where, on most evenings in the summer, a pianist or local accordion band provided music for dancing. Whenever possible during the summer months, I cycled to the Eels Foot Inn to hone my dancing skills with the young women waiting patiently in the refreshment room for their boyfriends or partners to withdraw from the bar. Occasionally, an unattached female provided an opportunity for me to try and perfect other skills, mostly without success as my efforts lacked confidence and usually resulted in a firm and curt rebuff.

Although we regularly used the facilities of our local public houses, neither my friends nor I drank to excess, due primarily to limited financial circumstances. When I was eighteen and a student in the sixth form at Great Yarmouth Grammar School, my parents gave me a pocket money allowance of 10s a week to cover all my personal expenses and entertainment. Any additional money had to be earned from paid employment at weekends or during school vacations. As a result, my introduction to the effects of excessive alcohol consumption did not occur until my first night at Leicester University. In an attempt to bond with my new student colleagues, I accompanied five freshmen from Beaumont Hall to the White Horse, a public house in the village of Oadby, where, our trouser pockets bulging with money (parting gifts from family and friends), we all proceeded to consume five pints of M&B, which turned out to be Mitchell & Butler's best bitter and not mild and bitter as I had expected. Until that time I had never drunk more than two pints of beer at a time and, inevitably, I discovered that alcohol not only induced vomiting but also apparently accelerated the rotation of the Earth. My four companions suffered a similar fate.

At the Village Hall

'At the Hop', Danny & the Juniors, 1958

In the 1950s, every village community aspired to possess a village hall or larger room where meetings, dances and film shows could be held. Many began as church or chapel rooms, controlled by a committee linked to that organisation, and held religious meetings and Sunday schools as well as general village activities. Others were established as memorial halls to commemorate those who lost their lives in the two world wars. After the Second World War many national and local government agencies provided loans and grants to help establish community halls in rural areas, which were then run as registered charities and managed by a committee elected from the relevant village community. The neighbouring village of Martham possessed a Memorial Institute, a long wooden building built in 1920 containing a large function room and two billiard saloons with tennis courts and a bowling green alongside. The construction of the Memorial Institute was partly financed by a local dignitary, Mr W. Bracey, in memory of Martham's dead in the First World War. Nearby Fleggburgh had a brick-built hall, which was developed in the 1940s by the National Council of Social Service under a post-Second World War village hall scheme and leased to the village for an annual rent. Rollesby was less fortunate. A church school, a small single-roomed thatched building located immediately behind the Horse & Groom public house, was donated to the village as a community hall in 1929 when a new larger council-controlled village school was built in a more centrally positioned site on the Main Road. When this hall, familiarly known as the Rector's Room, was destroyed by fire during the Second World War, no money was available to build a replacement. As a temporary measure, a small attic room above the stables at the Old Rectory was used as a substitute until the Rectory was eventually sold for development in 1950. Soon after the end of the war, a large green wooden shed-like structure, the 'Hut', was erected on the village playing field to serve as a changing room for the cricket and football teams, a refreshment room for the village fête and as a meeting place for the Ladies' Club as well as other village organisations. In 1953, a veranda was added which became a gathering place for many of the village youth, a cause of much discontent. Occasionally a hall from a neighbouring village or a room in Rollesby's primary school was hired to accommodate larger village functions such as fundraising dances and whist drives, wedding receptions and national celebrations, notably those for the Coronation. Eventually, in 1959 a new village hall was erected on the same site as the old church

The opening of Martham's Memorial Institute in 1920. During the 1950s it was the venue for film shows, whist drives, dances and socials. (Glenda Tooke)

school, financed jointly by a bequest from a former rector, funds raised by the Village Hall Committee and a grant from the Norfolk County Education Authority.

VILLAGE HALL PROPOSAL

At a well-attended public meeting at the school it was decided that a new village hall should be built on the site of the hall destroyed by fire during the war. It was explained that two funds, each of about £500 were available to form the nucleus of a building fund. A committee was appointed to draw up a scheme consisting of the trustees of the former hall, Captain D.G. Tacon, Col I.B.H. Benn, Mr H. Marsden-Smith, Mr C. Miller and Mr H. Haynes.

'Village News, Rollesby', *Yarmouth Mercury*, 1 April 1949

VILLAGE AMBITION REALISED

Rollesby's new £2,300 Village Hall – started in February and built in five months – was finally opened on July 4th by Norfolk's Chief Education Officer (Dr. F. Lincoln Ralphs). For 15 years the villagers of Rollesby have talked, planned and fought for a new hall. Many problems faced the project – one of which resulted in a special Act being passed – but on July 4th they saw their ambition realised and over one hundred villagers attended the ceremony. Mrs P.V. Tacon, wife of Captain D.G. Tacon, Chairman of the Village Hall Committee, read a message from her husband, who was ill, urging the villagers to make use of the hall and thanking the committee and the secretary, Mr W.F. Webb, for their work. The new hall stands on the site of the old school hall which was burnt down at the beginning of the war. It cost £2,300, a third of which came from an Education Authority grant, and the balance from the Rev. R.J. Tacon bequest and the Village Hall Fund. To enable the fund and the bequest to be merged an Act was passed at the end of last year. The hall will be the headquarters of every social organisation in the village. Mr C.A. Miller, Vice-Chairman of the committee, presided at the opening. Dr Ralphs was thanked by Mr. S.I. Gaze, the committee's treasurer.

Yarmouth Mercury, 7 August 1959

Even though Rollesby had no functional village hall for most of the 1950s, the facilities in Martham, Fleggburgh, Little Ormesby and Repps were a short fifteen-minute cycle ride away and, together with my family and friends, I regularly patronised the dances, drama productions, concerts, whist drives and film shows held at their various community halls. In my late teens, energised by the thought of females, I travelled to the more distant village halls of Potter Heigham, Ludham, Hoveton, Great Ormesby and Caister to attend dances, usually by cycle but occasionally on the back of Tim's Vespa motor scooter.

Almost every week a dance or social was held at one or other of the local village halls. So, on most Saturday evenings in my late teens, dressed in my best suit, white shirt, tie and polished shoes, my hair saturated with Brylcreem and swept back in a Tony Curtis style, I met with my friends at a local village 'hop'. A suit was essential,

The opening of Rollesby's new Village Hall in July 1959. (Stephanie and Barry Gallant)

even for those travelling by cycle with their trouser legs held away from the chain by clips. For most young men in the 1950s, an expensive suit, particularly one cut in an Italian style, was a personal statement intended not only to impress male companions but also potential female conquests. In my early teens, fashion was not an issue. My casual dress consisted mainly of redundant school uniforms – grey trousers, shirts, pullovers, socks and black shoes with laces. Until the age of thirteen, I mostly wore short trousers, a great source of personal embarrassment when in the company of girls. By the mid-1950s, I was certainly more fashion conscious and able to follow the current trends as my casual earnings during the school holidays increased, providing me with a modest surplus of cash with which to indulge my whims. I was definitely tired of grey and greatly admired the colourful clothing of the Teddy Boys, although I deplored their behaviour. I was also very much attracted to the off-duty casual wear of the many American servicemen who visited Great Yarmouth to drink and relax in the seafront bars. As a consequence, for casual wear I acquired colourful jumpers and canvas baseball boots, not always to my mother's liking. Many of my more garish Saturday purchases were returned by my mother and exchanged for a more subdued selection. I adored slip-on shoes and was amazed when we were given permission to wear them for school. Unfortunately, I preferred wearing slip-on shoes with colourful socks, not the normal sombre grey. For a while white socks were ignored but once the fashion was for lime green and shocking pink, the headmaster called a halt and introduced a ban on colour.

In reality, where fashion was concerned I was a novice. My first suit was bought for me by my Grandmother Miller as a fifteenth birthday present, a personally selected two-piece suit in a powder blue cloth with a red check, tailor-made by Burton's of Great Yarmouth. The jacket was double-breasted with two vents up the back and large pointed collars. A white handkerchief folded into a triangle inserted into the jacket's small top pocket added a touch of class The trousers, held up by a pair of my father's braces, had 24in bottoms, turn-ups and a buttoned fly. In cold weather I wore a grey pullover under the jacket, normally a home-knitted pullover with a cable stitch design. I have no doubt that I must have looked a comical sight in my creation but to my mind it was the height of elegance. Mother hated my suit and eventually bought me an off-the-peg charcoal grey two-piece, which served me for many years at interviews, formal occasions and dances. I even wore it at my wedding. My powder blue suit became redundant and disappeared, presumably consigned to a village jumble sale or the dustbin. My lady dance partners usually wore sleeveless pastel dresses with a high rounded neckline. The hemline was mid-calf and the skirt was puffed out by one or more layers of petticoats. A matching cardigan usually completed the ensemble, a necessity for colder evenings and romantic trips to the rear of the village hall. The closeness of modern ballroom dancing invariably provided me with a tantalising impression of the world beneath their dresses, a confusing world of conical bras, roll-on girdles, suspenders and stocking tops.

The author with his guitar, 1960. Casual fashions included sweaters, jeans (with turned-up bottoms) and elastic sided suede boots. (Author's Collection)

By the time I began my university course I had been converted to fashions dictated by teenage influences from America. My vests and baggy cotton trunks were quickly replaced by T-shirts and Y-front pants. At jazz sessions I wore shirt-length floppy Joe sweaters, corduroy trousers and brown winkle-picker shoes with elasticated sides or a pair of suede sand-coloured desert boots. I was converted to Levi and Wrangler blue denim jeans, faded and moulded to fit by being worn for an hour in a warm bath. No matter how much they shrank the legs were always too long for a short-legged person like myself and required a sizeable turn-up to fit. In my jeans, a tartan lumberjack coat and black cowboy boots, I fancied myself to be irresistible. My jiving partners were often dressed in tight calf-length jeans, a white blouse and a thick elastic belt around their waists.

On the whole, village dances were quite sedate affairs attended by a cross-section of the village community: young, old, farmer and labourer. However, the predominant age group was under thirty, as dances were one of the few occasions where young men and women could meet without comment. Mother once told me that she had first met my father at a dance in Potter Heigham, while many of my cousins also met their partners at dances. It was not unusual for couples to consolidate a mutually agreeable meeting locked together in a passionate embrace in the dark behind a village hall. Married couples mostly sat and danced together, while unattached females either perched on chairs around the room waiting for an invitation to dance from a fancied male, rejecting the advances of others, or danced with another female, taking it in turns to lead. Unattached men, often fortified by a pint or two at the local public house, normally stood in a gang at one end of the hall nervously looking for a partner. In the 1950s, dances were mostly modern ballroom dances such as the waltz, foxtrot and quickstep, with an occasional veleta, Gay Gordon or Saint Bernard's Waltz for variety. Spot and Excuse-me waltzes were used as an incentive to persuade reluctant performers to join in. The evening usually ended with energetic renditions of the hokey-cokey and 'Knees-up-Mother-Brown' followed by a romantic last waltz. Rock 'n' roll was not encouraged because jiving couples were a hazard in a crowded hall, often spiking the feet of other dancers with their stiletto heels or smacking heads with their flailing arms. However, my first introduction to rock 'n' roll was a demonstration during the interval at a Saturday dance in Martham. I watched the twirling couple with amazement, excited by the dance and the brief glimpses of stocking tops, knickers and suspenders. When the demonstration was over we were all given an introductory lesson in jive as part of the evening's entertainment. Music for dancing was usually provided by live bands made up from local musicians who performed unaided by microphones or amplification equipment. In Rollesby, two talented musicians, pianist Billy Allard and violinist Hilton Haynes, often provided the music for parties and socials, but for dances we were best served by two small accordion bands, Len Ebbage & his Band and Eddie Bates' Accordion Band (formerly known as the Rhythm Rascals). When a live band was unavailable, music was provided by dance band records played on a radiogram.

Socials (social evenings) were held to celebrate special occasions such as Christmas, New Year, the Coronation, the opening of Rollesby's new village hall or a

Eddie Bates and the Rhythm Rascals – Billy Crowe, Johnny Austin, Eddie Bates, Francis Whitehead and Hilton Haynes. Music for dances was usually provided by small local bands. (Eddie Bates)

village marriage. In nature, they were more of a party than just a dance and were attended by villagers of all ages, from the very young to the very old. Music was always provided for dancing, but individuals were encouraged to take a musical turn. Those who could sing, sang, and, even if strained or out of tune, were always enthusiastically appreciated. Normally a bar was provided for those who enjoyed a drink, and refreshments were served during the course of the evening – sandwiches, rolls, occasionally a plated salad, buns, cakes, and, sometimes, a pudding. Games were always played, usually team games involving the passing of an item down a line in which men and women took alternate places. A matchbox from nose to nose, an orange from under one chin to the next, a balloon from between one pair of legs to another and a polo-mint on a drinking straw from mouth to mouth. My favourite was always the key on a string. A key tied to a long piece of string was passed from man to woman alternately along the line of each team, down the man's trousers and out the bottom then down the front of the next woman's dress and so on down the line. Once all the members of each team were linked up in this way, the race was to see which team could return the key back the way it came in the quickest time. Inevitably, modesty took a back seat and my favourite memory of all is of the occasion when the key became snagged inside the trousers of our local milkman, who had not only passed it down his trouser leg but also inside his long johns. The vision of two ladies ferreting down the front of his trousers in an attempt to release the key remains a vivid memory to this day.

NEW YEAR'S EVE SOCIAL & DANCE

On New Year's Eve the Institute provided a scene for celebration and jollity on a scale seen in the village as rare and special occasions. The event organised by Mrs K. Francis, Mr Roy Francis and members of the Playing Field Committee was a social and dance, and there were so many novelties, games, dances, surprises and prizes that the 175 people who were admitted by ticket only were provided with a night of enjoyment to remember. Streamers and balloons were released from the roof and there were spot and competition prizes. Refreshments, with Mrs Alexander in charge, were available and a licensed bar was provided. The climax arrived at midnight when Mr Lyn Thomas, as Father Time, disappeared from the scene and Mrs L. Myhill emerged as Miss 1955. Music was provided by radiogram and Mr Roy Francis was MC. As a result of the evening's entertainment, £12 will be available for Playing Field funds.

'Village news, Martham', *Yarmouth Mercury*, 7 January 1955

On weekday evenings, various clubs and societies made use of the village hall facilities. Film shows were a regular feature at Martham, Great Ormesby and Fleggburgh and were normally well patronised before the advent of television. With my friend Tony, I cycled or occasionally walked to the Martham Institute or the Ormesby Church Hall to join the audience at a film show. The experience, however, was unlike any show seen at a commercial urban cinema. The room was usually set up with a large projector at one end and a small square screen on a stand at the other. In between, seats belonging to the village hall were arranged in neat rows. Audiences were drawn from villagers of all ages, usually families with children at the front and teenagers and courting couples toward the back. The show consisted normally of cartoons followed by a feature film and was a noisy affair. Apart from the soundtrack, which was often distorted, occasionally unintelligible and always loud, the action was accompanied by vocal encouragement from the teenage section, especially during romantic episodes, cries and screams from terrified or bored children, hearty cheers during the cartoons and a continual whirring noise from the projector. Periodically the film broke, necessitating a short break which was greeted with boos and then cheers when the film was restarted. My enthusiasm for film shows increased once I discovered girlfriends, as the auditorium provided a warm, dry and dark environment in which to develop my inter-personal relationships.

Clubs catering for young people, women and senior citizens were established in most Flegg villages during the late 1940s and early '50s, most holding their meetings in their local village hall or clubroom. Social clubs for men did exist in the villages, often providing an alcohol-free facility as an alternative to the bar of the local public house. In Fleggburgh, a men-only social club was based at the village Coffee House while Rollesby's men's club met in the rooms above the Old Rectory stables, each providing an opportunity for village males to meet, talk, smoke, sing and play cards, darts and billiards. By the middle of the 1950s, most of these clubs had closed due to a lack of interest, possibly another casualty of television.

A few villages also boasted energetic amateur dramatic societies. By 1950, youth clubs existed in Martham, Fleggburgh and Ormesby, although attendance was limited because, until 1959, all males over seventeen years of age were called up for National Service in the armed forces. Once Rollesby's village hall became operational in the autumn of 1959, a weekly evening youth club was established to provide the young people of the village with interesting games and activities, and as a more comfortable meeting place than the veranda of the hut or the Horse & Groom car park. Equipment for the club was mainly bought or donated by village residents – my father's contribution was his billiard table and two cues, a considerable sacrifice on his part. As well as games there were art classes and discussion groups. A small group of young guitarists provided music for dancing and gave me my first experience of singing in front of a band. Many villages ran scout and guide groups as well as youth clubs for their younger residents. My cousin Mary Crawford was a member of the 1st Martham Company of Girl Guides and proudly sewed her numerous efficiency badges onto her tunic. Like many of my friends, I was never tempted to join a cub or scout troop. The concept of scouting was considered old-fashioned among many teenagers, myself included, the emphasis on communal singing at their gang shows strange, and their instructors (adults in shorts) odd. Following in the tradition of my father and grandfather, both of whom had served in the army, I was more comfortable with my membership of the Army Cadet Force, albeit a reluctant member, because service as a cadet was a requirement for all Yarmouth Grammar School boys who were not members of the scouts.

Cousin Mary in her Guides outfit. During the 1950s, most teenagers belonged to a youth organisation. (Author's Collection)

GUIDES PARENTS' EVENING

The 1st Martham Company of the Girl Guides entertained their mothers and friends at the weekly meeting on Monday. The Guides gave displays of bandaging, making stretchers, Morse code, and also described the meaning of the company's colours. A camp scene was included. One new recruit, Valerie Hodds, was enrolled, and two second class Guides, June Brunson and Jean Derry, were presented with the cook's badge. The evening ended with the Guides forming a horseshoe around a model of the Guides badge and, each holding a lighted candle, sending greetings to Guides all over the world.

'Village news, Martham', *Yarmouth Mercury*, 13 April 1956

Village halls also became the base for many women's clubs, predominantly branches of the Women's Institute (WI) although there were a few Mother and Toddler clubs. In the 1950s, lively WI groups existed in Ormesby, Filby and Martham.

Without a village hall, provision for women in Rollesby was limited until the hut on the recreation field was connected to an electricity supply. Once the hut had heating, lighting and the power to boil a kettle, it became the home base for the Rollesby Ladies' Social Club, a club founded in 1949 with the aim of providing a meeting place for women where they could not only develop their interests and home craft skills but also provide assistance with village events and help for the elderly and infirm within the community. Both my mother and grandmother were enthusiastic members, and looked forward to the club's monthly meetings and occasional excursions.

Rollesby Ladies' Club on a day trip to meet their local MP, Anthony Fell, at the Houses of Parliament. For many villagers, club outings were their only break from daily chores. (Richard Tacon)

LADIES SOCIAL CLUB

At the first annual meeting a very successful year was reported. The club has over 30 members, two successful outings were organised and a Christmas Party. Members had rendered valuable assistance to village activities and the fête. The President, Mrs D.G. Tacon was re-elected, also Mrs M. Skinner the secretary who presented a balance sheet showing a good credit balance.

'Village news, Rollesby', *Yarmouth Mercury*, 10 March 1950

While Rollesby's Youth Club was a short-lived venture and the Ladies' Club was eventually replaced by a branch of the WI, the Happy Rollers, a club for the over-sixties, has endured and still thrives. Government concern for the welfare of senior citizens was championed in the late 1940s and early '50s by the WVS (Women's Voluntary Service) and as a result, between 1949 and 1953, almost every village in the Fleggs established a club for their elderly residents. Rollesby had the Happy Rollers, Repps the Merry Mardler's Club, Fleggburgh the Happy Autumn Club, Martham the Old Folks Club and Hemsby the Good Companions. The stated aim of all these clubs was to provide contact and companionship, support for the sick and information regarding state and other benefits available to old folk. Founded in October 1950, the Happy Rollers was a lifetime interest of my Aunt Doris Miller, who acted as club secretary and events organiser for many years.

OVER-SIXTIES CLUB FORMED

On Tuesday the WVS organised a party in the Church Hall to inaugurate an over-sixties club. After tea, provided by the WVS members and friends in the village, Mrs Cator of Ranworth Hall, gave a talk on organisation. There were games and singing, and entertainment was provided by Mrs Buck, Mr Haynes and Mrs Hinton.

'Village news, Rollesby', *Yarmouth Mercury*, 6 October 1950

Some village halls were equipped with a stage, providing a suitable venue for an amateur dramatic society. By the early 1950s, a number of drama societies had been established locally, in particular the Martham Players (founded in 1949), the Hemsby Village Revellers, the Filby Dramatic Society, the Ormesby Players, the Repps Revellers and the Fleggburgh Adult Drama Group, all within 5 miles or so of Rollesby. As well as pantomimes and plays, variety concerts were popular as they were less demanding than full-length plays and enabled individuals to perform to their strengths. These concerts usually consisted of short one-act plays interspersed with solo and group musical performances. My interest in amateur dramatics did not surface until I was at university. My only claim to fame before then was an appearance as a rook in a fundraising entertainment given by the pupils at Rollesby Primary School. However, some of my family were keen thespians. Uncle Arthur Cole was a talented actor and musician, and established a concert party and drama society in Great Yarmouth during the 1930s. Aunt Doris Miller was a member of the Fleggburgh Adult Drama Society and appeared in a number of their productions during the 1950s. Nevertheless, I was a keen and noisy member of the audience at many local pantomimes. Most productions were well attended and any errors, forgotten lines or below par performances by the players were all forgiven in appreciation of the fact that it was locals entertaining locals. Often, any profit from a production was shared with other village clubs. Most of the proceeds from a 1957 production of *The Crescent Moon* at Fleggburgh were donated to Rollesby's Happy Rollers Club as many of the cast, including Aunt Doris, were from Rollesby.

VARIETY CONCERT

The Adult Drama Group presented a variety concert in the Village Hall on Friday. A sketch 'The Lost Hat' was followed by duets by Mr & Mrs H.B. Tooke, another sketch 'Mother's Pride', songs by Brenda Notley, and a sketch 'Too many Brides'. The concert ended with a sing-song in which solos were sung by Mabel Barnes, Brenda Notley, Belle Tooke, James Gravin, Thomas Preece and George Moore. It was produced by Mr E. Taylor and Miss Edna Curtis was at the piano.

'Village News, Fleggburgh', *Yarmouth Mercury*, 2 May 1952

5

Playing Cards

LEARNING TO PLAY CARDS

'Jack o'Diamonds', Lonnie Donegan, 1958

During the immediate post-war period, everybody played card games. At least, without the distraction of daily television, everybody that I knew regularly played cards in the evening. There was not a household I visited that did not possess one or more packs of cards – the normal pack of fifty-two playing cards in four suits of thirteen: hearts, clubs, diamonds and spades numbered two to ten, Jack, Queen, King and Ace. We kept our cards in the right-hand drawer of the living room sideboard, often three or four packs at a time – one well-used pack for everyday use, held together by an elastic band, and other newer packs still in their boxes for use when friends or family came around. We were frequently given packs of cards as Christmas presents, often a box containing two identical packs, useful for games where two packs were required. As well as those for home use, my Grandmother Miller had a biscuit tin filled with fifty or more packs of cards for use in the fundraising whist drives that she organised.

ST DUNSTAN'S HELPED

A whist drive in aid of St Dunstan's in the Church Hall raised £6 10*s*. It was organised by Mrs N.B. Miller and Mr C. Miller was MC.

'Village news, Rollesby', *Yarmouth Mercury*, 3 March 1950

Most of our cards were of a standard size with geometric patterns on the back. Most public houses had packs of cards on the bar for their customers to use and, consequently, the reverse side was sometimes used to advertise beers, cigarettes, crisps and other products. I often played with sets that displayed adverts on the reverse: yellow backed cards advertising Gold Flake tobacco, navy blue-backed cards promoting Player's medium strength untipped cigarettes with the Player's logo (a lifebelt framing the head of a bearded sailor) in the corner, and the butler with a tray on the back of those advertising Kensitas tipped cigarettes. I was once given a present of a pack of cards with bathing beauties in swimsuits on the reverse, a prized possession that was proudly displayed and often used in card sessions with my male friends. One sixth former at Yarmouth Grammar School had a pack featuring female nudes on the back – a well-thumbed but rarely used set of cards. My father bought a circular set which was quite novel in appearance but the cards were difficult to hold. Well-used packs were regularly discarded, or given to children as playthings, as the more serious player could often gain an unfair advantage by remembering the value of a card from a blemish, tear or fold visible from the back.

I cannot remember when I first started playing card games. By the age of thirteen I was regularly playing cards with my father during dark winter evenings, mostly a simplified version of gin rummy. My father was a keen, enthusiastic and highly competitive player, and I quickly learned that there was never any likelihood that he would let me win. On those occasions when chance gave me the upper hand, I celebrated noisily, much to my mother's amusement and my father's embarrassment. When I could hold my own at rummy, he taught me to play six-card cribbage. For this he had a special board on which he recorded our scores for each hand using four small white pegs, a decorated brown varnished board with a central design of diamonds made by Jaques of London. On either side of the central design were sixty holes arranged in pairs of five in which he pegged the scores, up the inside and back down the outside, once round the board for sixty points and twice for one hundred and twenty. The first to complete two circuits was the winner. The ivory pegs used for scoring were stored in two holes at either end of the board, safely secured by a rotating metal lid. Despite my father's assertion that they were ivory, the pegs were most likely made from bone. Playing with my father taught me not only to think about the strategies to use in each game but also the technicalities of card playing – how to shuffle the cards, how to deal, to hold them fanlike in one hand sorted by suit and by value, and how to hide them from the view of other players or any overly interested spectators. Eventually I became proficient at shuffling by flicking the two halves of a pack together, placing one card from one half on top of a card from the other and so on through the pack, despite my father's complaint that this method bent the corners and spoiled the cards. It did, however, convey to my opponents the impression that I was an expert card player even if, in reality, this was untrue.

My Miller grandparents played cards on most evenings, usually against each other for a sixpenny wager which they placed in a round brass bowl on their portable card table. Their favourite game was German whist, a simple game for two. Thirteen cards were dealt to each player and the remainder of the pack was placed face down in a pile with the top card turned face upwards. The suit of the first card turned over denoted the trump suit for that game. The non-dealer then led a card which the other player had to follow, playing the same suit if possible but either trumping or discarding otherwise. The highest card won the trick as normal, unless it was trumped. The winner of the trick then took the upturned card and put it in his or her hand while the loser took the next. The process was repeated until all of the pile was used up. The game continued until all the remaining thirteen cards held in each of the hands of the two players were also played out, resulting in a possible twenty-six tricks in each round. Each player scored one point for every trick taken, the first to reach one hundred points won the game. Strategies employed during play often depended greatly on the value of the upturned card on the pile. Sometimes it was better to lose the trick and force your opponent to take the top card, hoping for a better one next in the pile. Among Grandmother Miller's collection of brass ornaments were a number of devices for indicating the trump suit in a card game, a useful reminder should anyone forget during play. One that she used regularly to indicate trumps was a miniature brass geographic globe about 4in high with the symbols for hearts, clubs, diamonds and spades on a rotating white band around the equator. The symbol of the trump suit would be turned so that it coincided with a line round the globe representing the longitudinal line through Greenwich.

I also played German whist, usually against my grandmother who, being less competitive than my father when playing with inexperienced young people, would explain the strategies to use in a game particularly when I was about to make a wrong decision. With both grandparents I played dummy whist. Although we were only three players, four hands were dealt, with the hand opposite the dealer being declared the extra 'dummy' hand. Once each player had sorted their hand, the dummy hand was turned face upwards on the table. The game then proceeded as normal partner whist with the dealer partnering the dummy and playing both hands, while the other two players played together against the dealer. In the next round the player on the dealer's left became the new dealer. Playing regularly with my family quickly gave me the ability successfully to play all forms of competitive whist.

Whenever four or more members of the Miller family were together – for tea or a family celebration – we always ended up playing whist, or variations of whist that, I suspect, may have been our own inventions. At Christmas parties we regularly managed three or four tables for normal partner whist, playing twelve hands as part of the evening's entertainment. Another variation, Contract whist, was a family favourite because the rules enabled any number of players to join in, although it was best played with four people. To start the game, as many cards as possible were dealt depending on the number of players, any left over remained on the table unseen. Each player had to declare publicly how many tricks they expected to win with the cards in their hand. The game was then played as for normal whist, hearts as trumps on the first round, then clubs, diamonds and spades, followed by a round with no trumps. At the end of each round, players scored one point for every trick that they won, with a bonus of ten if the total number of their tricks was the same as their prediction. In every subsequent round, one less card was dealt to each player until, in the last round everyone only had a single card to bid on. The winner was the person with the highest total number of points.

WHIST DRIVES

'He's got the whole world in his hands', Laurie London, 1957

Every week during the dark evenings from September until May there was always at least one whist drive to go to in the villages around Rollesby. Sometimes there were also afternoon drives attended mainly by retired older folk, mothers and housewives who did not have a full-time occupation. When Rollesby's new village hall opened in 1959, there were regular whist drives in Rollesby as well. By the age of thirteen, I was considered sufficiently competent at card playing to accompany my parents to whist drives. Sometimes we would cycle to the venue – the Martham Memorial

Institute or the Fleggburgh and Little Ormesby village halls – propping up our cycles against the walls of the building, other times my father would drive us there in his car which he parked on the road. Initially, I joined other children in the passage or a corner of the hall to read, draw or play games on our own. Sometimes I followed my parents around the room watching them play cards. Eventually, I was allowed to join in and play too.

Whist drives were very popular with the ordinary working folk of the villages and were used to raise funds for national charities, village clubs and for special village events. My grandmother was active in raising funds for St Dunstan's, a charity for the blind, and for the British Legion, particularly the Earl Haig's Poppy Appeal, and organised many whist drives on their behalf. This was a commitment that had begun after one of her brothers, Walter Mays, became a casualty on the Somme and died from his injuries during the First World War, a sacrifice commemorated with his name engraved on Martham's War Memorial. Other whist drives supported Rollesby's cricket and football clubs, provided the funds for the village children's summer seaside outing and the Christmas trip to the pantomime at Great Yarmouth. In Fleggburgh, whist drives were organised to raise the funds needed to purchase the village hall, at the Martham Village Institute they helped with fundraising to assist with buying the ground for a new recreation field and Repps' new village hall was furnished by proceeds from whist drives. It was not unusual for between one and two hundred players to attend a drive, travelling from neighbouring villages by cycle, car and in hired coaches that picked up at various designated points. The heyday of the whist drive was certainly the late 1940s and early '50s. The popularity of local drives decreased in the late 1950s as television became available and people became less inclined to venture out for entertainment, particularly on dark and cold winter evenings.

Village whist drives were an enjoyable social event and I continued to play at least once a fortnight until I left Rollesby for Leicester in 1959. I travelled around to different local venues, initially accompanied by my parents or grandparents but eventually, in my late teens, on my own, and got to know many of the other players by name, exchanged gossip and information and, more importantly, became aware of the strengths and weaknesses of individual players. In the countryside, whist drives were normally held midweek at various local village halls, coordinated so that there were few clashes with other village events, and there was always a drive to attend every week somewhere in the immediate neighbourhood. Whist drives were also popular in Yarmouth, organised by clubs and societies and advertised in the *Great Yarmouth Mercury*. Consequently, on a Tuesday, Wednesday or Thursday evening I regularly joined a queue of people outside the community hall of one of Rollesby's adjoining villages waiting to pay my admission fee for a whist drive. Normally two of the drive organisers sat at a table placed in the entrance to the hall, one taking the admission fee, usually 2*s* per person, and handing out scorecards, the other selling the inevitable draw tickets. Once inside it was essential to find a seat and a good card-playing partner for the first hand.

Inside, the card tables were arranged in a continuous loop around the hall. The tables themselves were rather rickety affairs with a 2ft 6in square playing surface, sometimes covered with green baize, on top of two pairs of thin crossed wooden legs.

No. of Deal	Trumps	Tricks Scored		Total	Signature	No of Deal	Trumps	Tricks Scored		Total	Signature
		Figures	Writing					Figures	Writing		
1	♥					13	♥				
2	♣					14	♣				
3	♦					15	♦				
4	♠					16	♠				
5	♥					17	♥				
6	♣					18	♣				
7	♦					19	♦				
8	♠					20	♠				
9	♥					21	♥				
10	♣					22	♣				
11	♦					23	♦				
12	♠					24	♠				

WHIST

Name
Commence at Table No . . . .
Lady/Gent

Total 1st. Half . . . . Total 2nd. Half . . . . Grand Total . . . .

One pair of legs was attached to the top while the other pair was freely hinged, secured by a clip underneath one side of the top, both pairs forming a cross under the table. At the end of the drive, the hinged legs were released and the table collapsed and folded up for ease of storage. The chairs were also collapsible with uncomfortable wooden seats. Once inside, the players arranged themselves four to a table, one person seated on each side of the table with opposite couples playing as a pair. Each pair consisted ideally of a man and a woman, with the men responsible for dealing. However, as whist was more popular with ladies – many men preferring to spend their leisure time in the local public house – some women played as men. Some of the stronger women players actually preferred to play as men as it was considered easier to win prizes as a man than as a woman, experience suggesting that women in general were the better whist players. The evening's play was controlled by a Master of Ceremonies (MC), usually one of the organisers equipped with a whistle if they did not have a very loud voice. The drive consisted of twenty-four hands of cards, twelve in each half. In the middle of the drive there was an interval of about fifteen minutes for tea, biscuits, a toilet break and gossip. The prizes for the evening's drive, together with the draw prizes, were normally displayed in a prominent position on a trestle table, usually on the stage if the hall had one or by the entrance door otherwise.

Once seated around the table (in order male, male, female, female) the man on the left counted the cards to ensure a full pack of fifty-two, shuffled them for the man on the right to cut and then dealt the individual hands in a clockwise direction. Trumps for the first round were always hearts, followed in the next round by clubs, then diamonds and finally spades, and then back to hearts again. The MC was responsible for ensuring that everyone knew which suit was the trump suit for that round. The lady next to the dealer played the first card of the game and the winner of that trick laid the first card for the next, and so on until the end of the hand. At the end of the hand, each couple counted the number of tricks that they had won and recorded this on their scorecard. Playing whist with my family had ingrained in my head a number of strategies for playing good whist and I continually recited these to myself during games. Lead away from a King, respond to your partner's lead, third player with an Ace and a Queen plays the Queen, if you hold five or more trumps lead trumps, count how many of each suit have been played, remember which court cards have gone. Despite a strict adherence to these rules, it never ceased to amaze me how many players had strange rules of their own, not always appreciated by their partners. Once play on all the tables had finished, the MC would blow his whistle, declare the trump suit for the next hand; a signal for the pair with the most tricks to move, the woman to the next table clockwise and the man to the next anti-clockwise. The man and woman with the least tricks remained at the table but split up as a pair and played with the arriving woman and man respectively. The losing man dealt the next hand.

On the whole, despite being well-organised occasions, most large whist drives had periods of total, often amusing, frequently frustrating, chaos. Everybody played whist, men and women, young and old, the expert and the novice. Some played in a lightning-quick fashion, others were slow and deliberate. Often proceedings were held up waiting for a slow table to finish a hand. Arguments were common, especially when a player had trumped their partner's trick, or led the wrong suit, often heated if opponents were accused of playing a wrong card, particularly if they had 'revoked' by laying a trump when they had a card of the suit being played. Progress was frequently delayed as individuals crawled around the floor looking for lost cards, occasionally tipping over a table in the process. In between hands, the gormless would wander aimlessly about the hall looking for their next table. All this was normally ignored by the MC, who would blow his whistle for the next hand to be played oblivious to the chaos happening around him. At the end of the drive scorecards were totalled up and the prizes were distributed – first, second and third man, first, second and third woman, highest first half score, highest second half score, lowest man, lowest woman. Each award was always accompanied by appropriate remarks and jibes, 'She always wins', 'He cheats you know', 'Booby prize again, he's useless, he scored two when he played with me'. The prizes were normally donated by individuals, local shops and village organisations; they were always objects, there were never any money prizes: a pair of blankets, a live pig, a tea set and a goose or a turkey at Christmas. Some village organisations held partner whist drives for those who preferred playing with the same person throughout the evening, thus avoiding the lottery of random partners. Occasionally a whist drive was nominated as a qualification drive, where the prize-winner with the highest score became eligible to enter a prestigious winner's drive usually held in Norwich. By the end of the 1950s, whist drives had become less popular, owing to competition from television and the advent of bingo, a game where success was totally based on chance and not skill, and the prizes were usually money.

FLEGGBURGH VILLAGE HALL

. . . the villagers are very interested in whist . . . out of the total population of about 600, attendances of 200 are by no means rare, and at a special Christmas drive there were 320 people from all over the area with coach loads from Reedham and Potter Heigham. There were so many people that overflows had to be accommodated in the men's club and school rooms. 'We give really good prizes and we find that it pays.' said Mr King (Secretary of Fleggburgh Village Hall Committee). When a reporter called to see the Rector, the Rev. R.A. Atkins, in the middle of the afternoon, he was acting as MC at a special whist drive for the women of the village controlling the scene with a whistle. Mothers played while the children amused themselves at the other end of the hall. Up to £40 had been raised from one whist drive he said, but that day the money would go to an old people's party to be held of course in the Hall.

In fact everything happens in the hall as on Thursday nights it is the village cinema, on Fridays it is used for the Youth Club and the adult drama group, which is very strong, use its stage, the Mothers' Union, the WVS and many other organisations meet there and it is the favourite place for wedding receptions.

'Village news, Fleggburgh', *Yarmouth Mercury*, 3 February 1950

OTHER CARD GAMES

'Gamblin' man', Lonnie Donegan, 1957

In addition to whist, I played many other card games, some whose rules I have now forgotten. By myself I played various forms of patience: canfield, spider and clock patience were the most popular. When I was old enough I played crib with my friends in the Horse & Groom public house, pegging our scores on a board with matchsticks. My Uncle Cecil Miller was particularly fond of solo which he played regularly in evening card sessions with family or friends in his home at the post office in Rollesby. Solo drives were often held at the Martham Village Institute but were never as popular as whist drives, perhaps because the game was more complicated than whist and required a level of competence beyond that of many card players. At parties my father always introduced a game he called Newmarket Race Day, a gambling game that he undoubtedly learnt when he was in the army. The four Aces were placed in a line to become the horses for the race. The rest of the pack was shuffled and the racetrack defined by the first six cards of the pack placed in a line in front of the Aces, each card indicating a step for the horses to take along the track. The dealer assumed the role of a bookie and declared odds for each of the horses, helped in deciding those odds by looking at the cards defining the racetrack. The Ace of the suit with the most cards lining the track would have the least chance of winning the race. After all the bets had been placed, cards were turned over slowly from the pack one by one; if the card turned over was a club, then the Ace of Clubs moved one step along the track, if a spade, the Ace of Spades moved and so on until one of the Aces completed the six steps and reached the finishing line at the end of the track. The progress of each horse was usually accompanied by cheers and encouragement from the punters.

Inevitably, at grammar school I was introduced to gambling games, in particular pontoon, three card brag and poker. Often at weekends six or more of my sixth form colleagues gathered at a designated venue to spend a long night gambling at cards and drinking beer. Not that we were serious gamblers or drinkers because our finances were very limited. One-penny stakes were the norm and a large bottle of Lacon's Light Ale each would last most of an evening. Occasionally our front room at Martham Road, Rollesby, became the venue for the card school and, as most of my Yarmouth friends did not have any personal transportation, it also became their uncomfortable sleeping quarters, although I think they spent most of the night talking in front of the fire. I, of course, spent the night comfortably asleep in my bed. Mother was always up early making tea, toast and Shredded Wheat in warm milk for our bleary-eyed lodgers before they made their way back to Yarmouth on the bus. Another regular venue was a boatyard next to Filby Bridge. I can clearly remember that on one occasion, tired of cards and fortified by more than our usual quota of ale, we all unadvisedly decided to skinny dip in Filby Broad at midnight. I soon discovered, not without an element of panic, that getting back into a high-sided rowing boat bobbing around at night in the middle of Filby Broad was not as easy as it might seem.

I was never tempted to join in any serious gambling games, although I played poker dice for pennies at Christmas with my uncles. I saw how easy it was to lose money at poker when I was employed at a Birds Eye pea-vining station in Upton. For a summer job in 1960, I joined a group of students and other odd personnel working permanent nights testing the quality of the pea harvest brought to the station for processing. The money was excellent although the work was hard. However, work normally ceased at about 3.30 a.m. in the morning and there was little else to do to pass the time away before the end of the shift at 6 a.m. other than to play cards or stare at the sunrise. Unfortunately, one of our team was a professional gambler working to pay off debts that he had incurred at poker. He was very adept at persuading the unwary, innocent or plain stupid among us to join him in early morning card sessions in the canteen. It quickly became obvious to me that playing poker with him and his like was a certain and quick way of losing money.

CARDS AT UNIVERSITY & BEYOND

'Whatever will be will be', Doris Day, 1956

At university I was introduced to contract bridge. Both my roommates in Beaumont Hall were bridge players and very soon our room became the venue for many late night bridge rubbers. Before university I had never played bridge and none of my family played bridge or considered it a suitable game to learn. Bridge was a game for the middle classes and not for working people. The middle class played bridge and golf, and watched rugby; the working class played whist and darts, and watched football. Richard's parents were the only people I knew who played bridge, at afternoon bridge parties or at the Conservative Club in Great Yarmouth. In 1959, Leicester University was still very much a middle class establishment and playing bridge was the norm. From the moment that it opened in the morning until it closed last thing at night, there was always a bridge game in progress in the Students' Union junior common room, often surrounded by a dozen or more spectators. Bridge was a serious business at university as some games were played for money, particularly those involving certain overseas students, especially those from the Middle East. It was inadvisable for any inexperienced bridge player to join a game played for money as the stakes, based on points scored, were often very high. Whether it was true or not, I remember clearly being told that one third-year mathematics student had lost all his term's grant in one day playing bridge. Poker games were also common throughout the day. A few hardened students, expert in the art of bluff and double bluff, purposefully added to their grant in fiercely contested poker games. Many new first-year students quickly learned that there were no friends to be made in love, war or in a game of poker.

With my student friends I also played Hearts, a game for four sometimes known as Black Queen or Dirty Lady, which we had adapted so that it could also be played with three or five players. The pack was never shuffled, even after a game, just cut before dealing. Most of the cards were dealt in fours, not one at a time as was normal. With four players, three fours and a single card to each player; with five players, two fours and two cards to each with the remaining two cards face down on the table and not in play; finally with three players, four fours and a single to each with the last card face down. Before starting the hand, each player passed any four cards to the person on their left. The game was then played as normal whist but with Hearts as the trump suit. The aim of the game was not to win tricks but to avoid taking any tricks that included the Queen of Spades or any cards from the suit of Hearts. These were penalty cards and penalty points were awarded against a player if any tricks won by that player included one or more of these cards: we awarded 5 penalty points for the Ace of Hearts, 4 for the King, 3 for the Queen, 2 for the Jack and 1 for the rest, 20 for the Queen of Spades. The game ended when the penalty points against any player reached 200, the winner being the one with the least penalty points at that time. If, in any round, a player managed to take all of the penalty cards within their tricks then their total penalty score was reduced to zero.

Regular card playing ceased for me during the 1960s once television had become the usual form of relaxation in the evening. Apart from a brief period when I joined a bridge playing group, my packs of cards have remained unused and relegated to the back of the sideboard drawer. I still enjoy an occasional game of spider patience, but now as a distraction on my computer.

6

On the Town

ORGANISATIONS, CLUBS & SOCIETIES

'Ready, willing and able', Doris Day, 1955

Part of my teenage leisure time was spent in Great Yarmouth and, to a lesser extent, Norwich, making use of their coffee bars, restaurants, sports facilities, dance halls, theatres and cinemas. The only problem for rural dwellers was transport. In an era when personal motor vehicles were a luxury, travel from village to town was mostly by public transport – the train or, as in my case, the bus. The ability to use the many entertainment opportunities offered by Great Yarmouth, especially in the evening, was usually determined by the timing of the last bus back home. Travel from Rollesby to Great Yarmouth and back was by a red number 5 Eastern Counties bus that provided an hourly service between the two locations. Other than Wednesdays and Saturdays, the last bus back to Rollesby left Great Yarmouth promptly at 9.05 p.m. Consequently it was not possible to attend any late-running evening functions other than on a Wednesday or Saturday unless alternative transport was available. For those who owned a car or could arrange a lift, this was not an insurmountable problem. Sometimes, for popular events, a local coach operator provided transport. Otherwise, villagers had to be satisfied with the entertainment available locally. I was fortunate, because during my late teens I was able to stay overnight with Grandma Cole at her home on North Market Road in Great Yarmouth. Yet, even in the town there were transport problems. Special buses had to be organised each weekend to transport the many late night dancers from the Floral Hall ballroom in Gorleston back to their homes in Yarmouth and Caister.

TRANSPORT REQUEST

A Martham coach operator, Mr J.R. Bensley, applied to the Traffic commissioners at Cambridge on Thursday for motor coach excursions to take village people to towns for recreation. He asked for excursions from Martham to Norwich for City football matches and to Yarmouth on two evenings for the Speedway and to the Wellington Pier. His application asked for two pickup points at Rollesby.

Yarmouth Mercury, 13 January 1950

While similar organisations, clubs and societies for residents of all ages existed in Great Yarmouth to those provided in the villages, the town offered a greater variety than was possible in the countryside. Many political, religious and working men's clubs had premises in the town and were often used by rural visitors. Grandfather Miller and Richard's parents were all regulars at the Conservative Club, while Uncle Stanley Cole was a member of the Liberal Club and even stood as a Liberal candidate in local elections. For the artistic there was the Photographic Society (founded in 1949), the Great Yarmouth Guild of Artists & Craftsmen and the Yarmouth Group of Artists. Every year I visited the exhibitions in the Central Library organised by members of the Yarmouth Stamp Collectors Club. There was even a long established Physical Culture Club, which frequently gave demonstrations of gymnastics at outside events in the summer.

For young people, in addition to the numerous youth clubs and scout, guide, brownie and cub packs, there were other organisations such as the Boys' Brigade, Girls' Life Brigade, the Air Training Corps and the Army and Sea Cadets. My cousin Francis Hammond was a member of the Boys' Brigade, an organisation whose theme song 'Sure and Steadfast', and the activities provided for its members (semaphore signalling, marching bands, rhythmic PT, football training, team games and camping) embodied the idea of fitness in body and mind. In 1954, I joined the Army Cadets, to be precise I joined Number 1 Company, 2nd Cadet Battalion of the Royal Norfolk Regiment, not out of choice but because membership was compulsory for pupils at Great Yarmouth Grammar School. Whether or not it was a necessary precaution at a time when war with Russia was a real possibility or, as suggested by the Headmaster, it was an activity ideal for developing a boy's character and leadership qualities, every Friday morning all senior boys at Yarmouth Grammar School were expected to stand on parade in the Upper School quadrangle impeccably dressed and ready for inspection in their khaki army cadet uniforms. Despite not being the most enthusiastic or the best turned-out cadet, I found the activities and tasks involved (map reading, weapons training and drill, field manoeuvres and rifle shooting) both enjoyable and interesting, a view not shared by some of the other boys.

SCHOOLBOYS AND THE CADET FORCE

Sir,
Imagine our intense amazement and disgust when our Headmaster announced prospective compulsory conscription into the School Cadet Force. We who have so far deliberately avoided the organisation on moral and other grounds which we do not consider altogether prudent to mention here, are to find ourselves forced recruits in a formation which we not only consider unnecessary but also repugnant. We doubt whether the present schooling in this Borough rewards the tax payer's money without suffering the monstrous indignity of devoting valuable school time, space and money to a force whose sole attraction has hitherto always been a means of escape from schoolwork. Operation 'Red Herring', in which the Grammar School cadets took a major part, obviously provided a considerable amount of free entertainment for those who witnessed it but why should we be coerced into becoming members of an organisation which provides the public at large with this and other ludicrous spectacles.
Yours faithfully, PUPILS

'Letters to the editor', *Yarmouth Mercury*, 13 July 1951

For those keen on drama, more opportunities existed for all levels of competence in urban Great Yarmouth than was possible in the rural villages. Beginners could develop their basic skills at training schools such as the Iris Castle School of Speech and Drama and the Great Yarmouth & District Stagecraft Club. A Great Yarmouth Festival of Drama was established in 1950 to encourage drama in the Borough through a competition in which local schools, youth and adult drama groups competed against each other by presenting short one-act plays for assessment by a panel of adjudicators. As well as my Aunt Doris Miller, many of my Cole relatives were involved with dramatic and musical productions. Uncle Arthur Cole was both director and producer for numerous shows in Great Yarmouth and Birmingham. My cousins, Barbara and Terry Cole, were cast in many acting parts with both their school and adult drama groups, including some leading roles. Those talented enough to progress beyond amateur drama at the local village halls or their urban counterparts could develop acting skills as members of the very successful Yarmouth Amateur Operatic & Dramatic Society. For most of the 1950s, this society staged three productions every year: a musical, a play and the popular and well-supported Christmas pantomime. The seafront Windmill Theatre was the usual venue for the play and the larger Wellington Pier Pavilion Theatre was home to the pantomime and musical. Each year, Rollesby villagers raised funds through whist drives and other activities to organise a trip to the pantomime for all the village children

aged under thirteen. Armed with an orange and, once rationing had ceased, a bag of sweets, we marched to the end of the Wellington Pier to become a noisy but appreciative part of a young and excited audience. In my later teens I continued to attend, often as a guest of my Aunt Doris and the Happy Rollers Club. An added attraction for all of us was Linda Taylor, once a resident of Rollesby, who had progressed through the ranks of the society to become one of its leading ladies, eventually starring as Cinderella in the 1958 production. The Flegg village communities were always extremely supportive of any homegrown talent, no matter what field their achievements were in.

Uncle Arthur Cole and cousin Barbara in costume. Amateur dramatics were a popular pastime in both town and country. (David Riley)

PANTOMIME VISIT

Rollesby Over 60s Club held its annual trip to Yarmouth Pantomime on Saturday afternoon when members enjoyed 'Beauty and the Beast' presented by the Yarmouth Amateur Operatic & Dramatic Society. They had a special interest in this show as Linda Taylor until two years ago lived at the White House Farm, Rollesby. After the show members enjoyed a hot meal at 7 Nelson Road South. The secretary Mrs D.C. Miller was thanked for her efforts and presented by Mrs J. Moore with a bouquet.

'Village news, Rollesby', *Yarmouth Mercury*, 11 January 1957

1950	*Aladdin*	1956	*Humpty Dumpty*
1951	*Cinderella*	1957	*Beauty & the Beast*
1952	*Robinson Crusoe*	1958	*Cinderella*
1953	*Robin Hood & the Babes in the Wood*	1959	*Red Riding Hood*
1954	*Jack & the Beanstalk*	1960	*Dick Whittington*
1955	*Mother Hubbard*		

Pantomimes performed by the YAODS, 1950–60.

While the pantomimes flourished, particularly through the skills and efforts of committed members such as Derek Marshall and Jack Bacon, audiences for the plays diminished as television became a more popular entertainment in the evening. Not only amateur drama societies, but also many professional repertory companies suffered a similar fate. A company based at the Little Theatre, a small theatre at the rear of the Royal Aquarium on Great Yarmouth's seafront, was forced to cease all year-round productions by the end of the 1950s due to diminishing audiences.

TV VICTIM

So TV has claimed its first live theatre victim in Yarmouth. At the last performance at the Little Theatre on Saturday evening Mr Anthony Cundell, the producer, made no bones about it. TV had so reduced audiences this winter that they could not carry on, he said, and what with that and the burden of entertainment tax they were forced to close down. Thus after a period of ten years the town is without a regular repertory theatre, open winter and summer alike.

'Round and about by Scout', *Yarmouth Mercury*, 7 December 1956

COFFEE BARS & RESTAURANTS

'Smoke gets in your eyes', The Platters, 1959

A feature of the 1950s was the growing popularity of coffee bars, places where young people in particular met to talk and socialise while drinking cups of frothy espresso coffee in shallow opaque plastic cups with miniscule handles. At home, I rarely drank coffee – our drink of choice was tea, proper tea brewed in a large brown teapot, with the pot and its contents kept warm by one of mother's colourful hand-knitted tea cosies, tea made from Brooke Bond Dividend or Typhoo tealeaves that were kept in a caddy beside the kettle in the scullery. We drank tea after every meal, not just one cup but two or more with at least two spoonfuls of sugar in each cup. My father drank his tea from a large blue and white half pint mug. On Sundays, we drank tea at 11 a.m. with biscuits, and at 4 p.m. with cake. When visitors came round we offered them tea. At the end of the day we had tea and biscuits before we went to bed. My father and I had a habit of dunking biscuits in our tea, especially ginger and chocolate wholemeal biscuits. Sometimes we even dunked our teatime buns, shortcake and slices of sponge. Mother frowned on this habit until the newspapers revealed that Princess Margaret also dunked her ginger biscuits. An essential treat for Grandmother Miller on her monthly shopping expeditions to Yarmouth or Norwich was to take tea in a teashop, café or hotel lounge, a ritual involving tea served on a tray by a waitress in a black dress and a white apron. On the tray was a metal pot filled with hot tea, another pot filled with boiling water, a silver milk jug and sugar bowl, a strainer in a holder and an appropriate number of teacups, saucers and spoons. Sometimes she ordered sandwiches that arrived cut into triangles, often without their crusts – ham, cucumber, fish and shrimp paste or potted meat. But she always ordered pastries which were served either on a plate with a metal handle screwed into its centre or direct from a mobile trolley. On the few occasions when I accompanied grandmother on a shopping trip I looked forward to this treat of tea and cakes, and invariably selected my favourite pastry, a round sponge with a white cream topping surrounded by green marzipan leaves that looked incredibly like a small cauliflower.

    Although my parents preferred tea, I drank coffee regularly at Rollesby post office with my Aunt Doris Miller. Every morning except Sunday, Aunt Doris made coffee at 10.15 a.m. to coincide with Uncle Cecil Miller's return home from his early morning delivery of newspapers and groceries. This was such a well-known event among her family that I was not the only one of her teenage nephews who mysteriously arrived just as coffee was being served. Naturally, although we enjoyed her company, being teenagers there was always a hidden agenda. Aunt Doris was a heavy smoker of Players un-tipped cigarettes. She was a generous smoker and always insisted that her guests smoked along with her, even though we invariably had no cigarettes of our own to offer back. Although the cigarettes were a definite attraction, her coffee was an acquired taste, as it was made from a thick black liquid that she dispensed from a bottle labelled Camp Coffee. One teaspoonful for each cup was ladled into a saucepan, mixed with the appropriate amount of milk, stirred and brought to the boil. The resulting cups of purplish-looking coffee were quite palatable with numerous spoonfuls of sugar, but invariably came with a thick skin floating on the top. Coffee time regulars became quite adept at removing the skin with their fingers or a spoon, thus avoiding the indignity of swallowing a mouthful of gunge.

    From the mid-1950s, meeting friends in coffee bars became part of teenage culture. Most Saturday mornings I met with six or more of my grammar school colleagues in the Kenya coffee bar located above Purdy's bakery shop next to

Brucciani's coffee bar and ice cream parlour, Horsefair Street, Leicester, 1960. A popular meeting place for students and teenagers as well as the weary shopper. (© Leicestershire County Record Office)

Palmer's department store in Great Yarmouth. Although it was intended as a refreshment facility for tired shoppers, the coffee bar had become a gathering place for numerous groups of noisy teenagers, much to the dismay of many ladies carrying heavy shopping bags. We normally occupied one of the café's half-dozen or more tables for at least an hour, discussing topics of interest while consuming a single cup of espresso coffee. Although the small shallow plastic cups contained little more than two good mouthfuls of liquid, the contents were a definite improvement on Aunt Doris' Camp Coffee. At university, coffee replaced tea as my main hot drink in the evening, mainly because it was easier to make and there was no coffee equivalent to tealeaves. It also had the added bonus of helping me to keep awake longer while studying or socialising with student friends. During the daytime, I spent many hours in the Students' Union coffee bar drinking and talking with other students, often when I should have been elsewhere, either at lectures or working in the library. In town, I consumed many cups of coffee either at Brucciani's coffee shop on Horsefair Street, a modern, neon-lit establishment with plastic seats and screwed-down tables, or at a continental café near to the clock tower, a favourite haunt of Leicester's many foreign students, where I spent many happy hours discussing authoritatively the merits of various continental films that I barely understood.

Although we enjoyed our food, my parents and I hardly ever went to a restaurant for our meals. Going out to dinner was not something that we did, possibly because it was far too expensive for any of us to afford on a regular basis. In an effort to impress, I once treated a girlfriend to lunch. This was an event I never repeated as, to my horror, at the end of the luncheon I was presented with a bill that took away most of my weekly pocket money. We frequently visited friends and relatives for a meal, but we usually went for tea not dinner. As I recall, Christmas dinner with my Miller grandparents and the formal annual football and cricket presentation dinners were the only regular exceptions to this rule. On the rare occasions when we did eat out as a family, it was always as part of a special event – an outing to Great Yarmouth for a show, a trip to the races or a get-together with visiting relatives – and then we normally ate a fish and chip supper at Nichols' Restaurant on Theatre Plain. Most days, mother cooked, as she considered it to be her responsibility and, perhaps, one that my father and I took for granted. Luckily mother enjoyed cooking and we certainly enjoyed the results. Once I had grown out of my childhood fads – at one time, I would never eat anything that was yellow – I ate anything and everything that she cooked. I even enjoyed school lunches.

The top table at Rollesby Cricket Club's annual dinner in 1951. Officials pictured are Capt. D. Tacon, Mr and Mrs F. Moore and Col. I. Benn (Club President). The preferred dinner drink is bottled beer and not wine. For many villagers, club dinners were their only meals eaten out. (Carrie Spencer)

For my family, eating out meant a fish and chip supper, often in Nichols' Restaurant on Theatre Plain, Great Yarmouth. (Colin Tooke)

Mother was an excellent cook – maybe in the 1950s she had to be. Without the benefits of refrigerators, freezers, pre-prepared and take-away meals, most of our food was cooked fresh every day from raw ingredients. The only pre-prepared items that she was able to use came in tins. The only take-away meal was fish and chips from the shop on Martham Green or the Saturday night visit of the chip van to the Horse & Groom car park. A cooked dinner was served at 5.30 p.m. during the week and at 12.30 p.m. at weekends. During school term times, I ate two cooked meals every day. The weekly menu was determined by the Wednesday and Saturday visits by the butcher's van. On Saturday, mother bought a large joint of meat for our traditional Sunday roast lunch, usually beef, lamb or pork, but, occasionally, she purchased a chicken, which was considered to be a special treat. Monday's dinner was invariably the roast again served cold with potatoes and vegetables and on Tuesday she often used the remainder of the meat to make either a stew with large round fluffy white dumplings, or a hotpot or a meat patty. On Wednesday she frequently bought chops or, as a special treat, the ingredients for one of her keenly anticipated steak and kidney puddings, made in a white bowl with a pastry top and cooked with a muslin cover tied over the top of the bowl. For variety she often bought fish from the fishmongers in Yarmouth, fresh herrings which she served covered in oatmeal and fried in a pan, or kippers and bloaters. In the summer she made egg, cheese, sardine, shrimp or ham salads with the salad ingredients picked straight from the garden. Although her weekly menus varied, Friday was always fish and chips brought home by my father on his return from work, often after an early evening visit to the barbershop in Martham. Saturday lunchtime was routinely eggs, sausages, bacon and fried onions. We always had a pudding with our Sunday meal but on other days we had pudding only if there was something left to eat up or if fresh fruit was available from the garden. Mother's puddings were a treat – suet pudding with treacle, large cooking apples cored and baked in the oven with sultanas, apple, blackberry and raspberry pies, stewed pears and plums – all served with big helpings of yellow custard.

Things changed drastically when I left home for Leicester. My total ignorance of cookery ensured that most of my meals were mass-produced at the Beaumont Hall refectory, the Percy Gee Students' Union restaurant or various cafés, dining rooms and cheap restaurants in Leicester city centre. My few efforts at cooking, usually fish fingers or beef burgers with eggs, were such disasters that when I had no money for eating out, I often went hungry. Nevertheless, by eating out I was able to sample new foods and dishes never experienced in rural Rollesby. On most Sundays, I joined several other students at the Blue Lagoon Restaurant on Waterloo Street where I always had a Vienna steak. I became addicted to savoury as well as sweet pancakes served in a specialist restaurant in Leicester's city centre. I was introduced to Chinese cuisine and had my first curry in 1960 at the newly established Taj Mahal Indian Restaurant on Highfield Street, a popular late night venue for students and other inebriates returning home from a Saturday night dance. Undoubtedly we were made to suffer for our ignorance of what constituted good Indian food as, no matter whether we ordered a plain curry, Madras or Vindaloo, the dish was usually so hot and spicy that our mouths and throats burned as we hastily shovelled down our meal without tasting it. I have no recollection that the restaurant provided a takeaway service. I certainly did not eat takeaway curries, Chinese meals or pizzas in my student accommodation. Fish and chips were still the only dish that I bought from a shop and ate in my flat.

GOING TO THE CINEMA

'Western Movies', The Olympics, 1958

Going for a night out in Great Yarmouth normally meant going to the cinema. Before the arrival of our first television set, going to the pictures was a regular event, not only for me but also for my parents. In the early 1950s, watching films at the cinema was the popular choice of most families for an evening out, including my own family. Consequently, every town possessed at least one cinema or picture house to cater for this demand. In Great Yarmouth we had the luxury of five cinemas to choose from – the Regal, Regent, Aquarium, Empire and Windmill – more than most other towns of an equivalent size. Positioned equidistant along Regent Road and

the Marine Parade, areas associated with the holiday trade, these cinemas catered for the annual summer influx of holidaymakers as well as for the local population. Built in 1908 opposite the Wellington Pier on Marine Parade, the Windmill, originally called the Gem, was not only the first cinema in Great Yarmouth but also the first purpose-built picture house in the country. This was followed in 1911 by the building of the Empire, also on Marine Parade, and, in 1914, the conversion of the Royal Aquarium from an Edwardian sea life centre into a cinema. Finally the Regent was established in 1915 and the Regal in 1934, both on Regent Road. A sixth cinema, the Plaza, located on the Market Place, was opened in 1915 and traded until the outbreak of war in 1939 when it became a storeroom for Woolworth's.

The Regal Cinema, Great Yarmouth. Before the arrival of our first television set, going to the pictures was a weekly event for my family. (Colin Tooke)

All five cinemas were impressive buildings, each having a flight of steps leading up to a large entrance hall with a ticket kiosk on one side and a sales counter selling confectionary, drinks, ice cream and magazines on the other. To either side of the entrance doors were cabinets displaying photographs of the stars and scenes from current and forthcoming films. Inside, 500 or more customers could be seated on uncomfortable tip-up seats in front of a single large screen, usually on two floors – the ground floor stalls and a smaller upper circle. Seats in the upper circle were the most expensive and those at the front of the stalls the cheapest. Owing to its popularity, going to the cinema usually involved queuing, especially for weekend shows. Seats could not be booked in advance and there were no set times for admission. Cinemagoers had to wait until places became available, normally during an interval at the end of a film or, occasionally, partway through a showing as earlier customers vacated their seats. Tickets were not allocated to any specific seats, only to an area of the cinema defined by price. Nor were customers prevented from entering or leaving at any time. Some even remained in their places to see the main film through twice. Consequently, concentration was frequently broken by the squeaking of seats, people standing up and sitting down again as new customers attempted to locate a seat in the darkness while a film was in progress, accompanied by the grumbles and mutterings of those around them. At busy times, uniformed usherettes equipped with a torch guided customers to empty seats. Complete programmes lasted between 3 and 3½ hours and ran continuously from midday until 10.30 p.m. in the evening. Each complete programme consisted of two films: the main feature film, which was supported by a short cheaply made B movie together with adverts, trailers for forthcoming films, cartoons and news reports. During the intervals between films, usherettes appeared in the gangways selling ice creams and drinks out of a tray supported by a strap hung around their necks. At the end of the final show, everybody rushed out to avoid standing for the National Anthem.

My mother was a keen picturegoer and during the early 1950s went to the cinema at least once a week. During the school holidays, I frequently accompanied her to Great Yarmouth on a weekday-shopping trip that normally included an afternoon at the cinema. In the autumn and winter, my parents and I went to a film show on most Friday nights, travelling to Yarmouth in my father's car. In the summer he was always far too busy at work or tending the market garden at the Field to go to the pictures. In terms of the time, our picture going was not excessive. Aunt Edith and Uncle Frank Hammond went to the cinema three times during most weeks, their commitment betrayed by the piles of film magazines in their front room, mostly monthly editions of the *ABC Film Review* and *Picturegoer*. As a family, our preference was for comedies, films that included the zany adventures of Bob Hope and Bing Crosby in the Road films (frequently accompanied by Dorothy Lamour in a swimsuit), Bob Hope with Jane Russell in *The Paleface* and *Son of Paleface*, the Girls of St Trinians and the idiotic antics of Norman Wisdom in *Trouble in Store*, to mention just a few. My father particularly enjoyed the Doctor series, delighting in the performances of the pompous James Robertson Justice. At fifteen years of age, I enjoyed the Doctor series because of Brigitte Bardot's appearance in *Doctor at Sea*. Without my father, mother and I preferred to watch adventure stories, westerns and war films. Together we watched John Wayne win the Pacific war single handed in *The Sands of Iwo Jima*, Jack Hawkins' stiff upper lip in *The Cruel Sea*, Alan Ladd trying to be a tall hero in *The Red Beret*, Faith, Hope and Charity defending the skies in *The Malta Story*, and Barnes Wallace's bouncing bombs in *The Dam Busters*. On my sixteenth birthday, as a sign of my growing independence, I paid for my mother to see the heroic true story of Douglas Bader in *Reach for the Sky*, a film she regarded as her absolute favourite, identifying with the legless Bader because he flew most of his Battle of Britain sorties from a local RAF station in Norfolk. In common with many soldiers who served in the war, my father had little time for war films.

Despite most films being produced in colour and the excitement offered by experiments with 3D vision and widescreen cinemascope, once they had a television set my parents preferred to watch programmes at home on a small flickering screen rather than venture out to the cinema. But for me the cinema still maintained its attraction, particularly as in the late 1950s many films appeared to reflect the tastes and interests of younger people. As a child I was a member of the ABC minors and every Saturday morning I joined the noisy throng at the Regent cinema to watch cartoons, short westerns and the serialised adventures of Tarzan and Buck Rodgers. In my teens I joined the young people who travelled on the afternoon bus to Great Yarmouth every Sunday during the winter months for a film and a fish and chip

ABC Film Review *magazine and* Picturegoer *covers from the 1950s.*

supper before catching the 9.05 p.m. bus back home. In my late teens, the cinema was the natural location for a first date with a girlfriend.

The cinema was not only a prime form of entertainment but also a major source of knowledge and information. Additionally, it was a great influence on the way many individuals thought and behaved, especially teenagers like myself. The cinema provided me with a background in English literature and history, although all too often it was an imperfect Hollywood version. Occasionally the senior boys of Yarmouth Grammar School were taken en masse to the cinema to watch one of the classics on the big screen. With the school I attended special showings of Laurence Olivier's *Henry V* and Marlon Brando in *Julius Caesar*. *Pathé News* brought reasonably up-to-date information to the public in the same way that television news does today. There were also a number of factual films and documentaries, a relatively new innovation for the cinema of the 1950s. I adored the two documentaries about the Coronation – *Elizabeth is Queen* and *A Queen is Crowned* – both of which I saw twice and, by association, the film detailing the climbing achievements of Edmund Hillary and Tenzing Norgay in *The Conquest of Everest*. Often, the B film was an episode from a police drama series introduced by Edgar Lustgarten re-enacting actual cases investigated by Scotland Yard. Like many others, I marvelled at Walt Disney's first feature-length natural history film *The Living Desert* and its follow-up *The Vanishing Prairie*. I was also amused rather than titillated by *Around the World With Nothing On*, a film featuring the Duke of Bedford in which he extolled the virtues of nudism, illustrated by tasteful but often comical images of nudists at Woburn Abbey and various islands in the Mediterranean. I remember Tim and me collapsing into hysterical laughter at the sight of a large fat nude gentleman riding a bicycle. Our cinema heroes guided our fashions. Although I was too old to consider a Davy Crockett raccoon hat, my hairstyle was deemed to be a Tony Curtis. Marlon Brando and James Dean were idolised although I personally never tried to emulate their storyline characters. Some did follow their examples. A student friend spent most of his time at university adorned in leather jacket, trousers and peaked cap, and travelled into campus on a motorbike. Films like *The Man with the Golden Arm*, *Blackboard Jungle* and *Saturday Night and Sunday Morning* challenged our attitudes towards sex, drugs and violence. But more than anything, the cinema championed rock 'n' roll, the music of the young. I shouted, yelled and occasionally jived in a cinema's aisles to the music in films like *Rock Around the Clock*, *Don't Knock the Rock*, *Jailhouse Rock*, *6-5 Special* (the film) and even *Expresso Bongo*.

At university I continued to be an avid picturegoer, watching films at least once a fortnight. My favourite cinema in Leicester was the Cameo, a small establishment on the High Street that specialised in fringe and continental films. I spent many evenings on the back row of the Cameo with a girlfriend occasionally watching a film. On one unforgettable evening, the lights came up at the end of the show to reveal that the occupant of the next seat was one of my lecturers with his arm firmly stuck up the jumper of his female companion. My first official position at university was as bookings secretary for the Leicester University Film Club, a post that required me not only to book films but also to produce a brief critique of each film to be shown at the fortnightly meeting. My critiques, typed onto A4 paper and painfully reproduced on a spirit duplicator, were hardly ever read but were turned into paper aeroplanes by a rowdy audience and propelled into the projector beam, amid cheers of delight as the shadow of a paper plane crossed over the screen. Despite these juvenile antics, the film club introduced me to classical films such as Bergman's *Seventh Seal* and *Wild Strawberries*, the Wajda trilogy *A Generation*, *Kanal* and *Ashes & Diamonds*, and Akira Kurosawa's *Seven Samurai*. Since the mid-1960s, going to the pictures has become a rare event. Like many, I usually wait for current films to become available on video or DVD, or to be shown on television. Watching films has ceased to be the sociable activity that it was for me in the 1950s and is now one that I normally do at home.

GOING DANCING

'Save the last dance for me', The Drifters, 1960

In the 1950s most people could dance – it was generally considered to be an essential social skill. Dancing was not only an enjoyable and healthy activity; it was also a means of mixing with and meeting other people. Consequently, I was encouraged to dance from an early age. At primary school I was taught folk and country dancing, while mother taught me modern ballroom dancing in our living room. Dancing classes were held in many of the Flegg village halls, often as one of the activities of the local youth club, and included instruction not only in modern ballroom and country dancing but also in acrobatic, tap and ballet.

DANCING DISPLAY

The Village Hall was packed on Friday evening for a dancing display by Miss Rita Nicholls' pupils. Children from Rollesby, Caister, Ormesby and Fleggburgh took part. Tickets and programmes had been sold by members of Fleggburgh Youth Club for the Village Hall funds.

'Village news, Fleggburgh', *Yarmouth Mercury*, 21 May 1950

In Great Yarmouth children of all ages, although mainly girls, were taught ballet, rhythmic and tap at various Schools of Dancing, including those that were organised by dance instructors such as Jean Boulton, Joy Manser, Rita Nicholls and Phyllis Adams. Every year all the schools demonstrated the skills and achievements of their pupils in public displays of dancing, often held at the Wellington Pier Pavilion. I remember accompanying my mother and Aunt Doris Parnell to watch my cousin, Deanna, take part in a display by the Phyllis Adams' School. Not that I was particularly interested in watching lines of children of all shapes and sizes rhythmically tapping away in apparently over-large shoes with big bows, or prancing over the stage in a tutu. My aunt and my mother, on the other hand, spent most of the show cooing over their performances and pointing enthusiastically at the brief appearances of my cousin. For teenagers and adults, regular well-attended classes in modern ballroom dancing were held at various dance halls and hotel function rooms, usually in the hour preceding a formal dance. Each year, the Hall Mackenzie

Phyllis Adams School of Dancing

★

DANCING DISPLAY

by Pupils of the above School

Britannia Pier Pavilion

Saturday, October, 20th

at 3 p.m.

★

Seats bookable by Programme at Messrs. Jarrolds

Programme 9d.

Above: *Dancing Display, 1951.*
Right: *Cousin Deanna in her ballet costume, ready to perform at the Phyllis Adams School of Dancing, 1951.* (Author's Collection)

School of Dancing advertised classes in Old Time, Rumba and Samba, Waltz and Quickstep, Foxtrot and Tango. Jive and Latin American classes were added in 1956 and, in 1958, instruction in Cha-Cha dancing.

For those able to travel to Great Yarmouth, opportunities for dancing existed on most nights of the week at various establishments throughout the town. The main venues for dancing in winter as well as summer, catering for up to 1,500 dancers each, were the Britannia Pier Ocean Ballroom with its resident band, Charles Bosomworth and the Oceanaires Dance Orchestra, the Floral Hall in Gorleston with the Eddie Gates Orchestra, the Wellington Pier Winter Garden Ballroom with Bert Galey's Orchestra and, from 1958, the New Gari Ballroom with the Gordon Edwards Sextet and Rollesby's ex-resident, Linda Taylor, as the female vocalist. A few larger hotels also provided regular public dances – the most popular of these among younger dancers was The Goode's Hotel on Great Yarmouth's seafront. For most of my early teens, my dancing was limited to dances and socials at local Flegg village halls or the refreshment room at the Eels Foot Inn. Sometimes I cycled with my village friends to Drake's Dance Hall in Potter Heigham, a wooden building adjacent to the Bridge Hotel alongside the river, where we supped a half of shandy while sizing

In the early 1950s, cousin Margaret gave dancing exhibitions with this troupe from Joy Manser's School of Dancing in concert parties held at various church halls, Great Yarmouth's Wellington and Britannia Piers, and the Gorleston Super Holiday Camp. (John and Margaret White)

up the female talent holidaying on the Broads. In my later teens I joined many of my sixth form colleagues to dance mainly at the Floral Hall Ballroom, staying overnight with Grandma Cole in Great Yarmouth. In the 1950s the Floral Hall was a typical ballroom with a circular shiny sprung wooden dance floor, a stage area to accommodate the band, a raised seating area surrounding the dance floor and bars on the opposite side to the band. Saturday night was Popular Modern Dance Night when men and women of all ages met to dance the light fantastic. Jiving was discouraged. Some ballrooms displayed signs indicating that jiving was banned.

WHY NOT JIVING?

Sir, why are the older generation so dead set against jiving? When they complain of it, do they ever stop to think of how some of them went crazy over the Charleston in the twenties, which, in our opinion, must have been equally as bad or even worse? In Yarmouth and Gorleston there is no dance hall in which we can jive. In a previous letter we were told to go to Lowestoft. Why should we go there when we have dance halls in our own town? Lowestoft has both a jazz club and a dance hall where jiving is allowed. Why doesn't Yarmouth keep up with the time? The old days are over; this is the modern world where jiving is gradually taking the place of the more sedate type of dancing.
Two jive lovers.

'Letters to the editor', *Yarmouth Mercury*, 8 July 1955

The lack of transport often limited my ability to attend special dances in Yarmouth or elsewhere. In January 1959, the annual Policemen's Ball, a major event locally, was held at the Seacroft Holiday Camp in Hemsby. Encouraged by a friend at Yarmouth Grammar School, who boasted that he would be able to borrow his father's car, I bought two tickets for the ball, one for me and the other for my then girlfriend who lived in Ludham. The arrangement was that we would be picked up by car near to Ludham Church at 7 p.m. and driven to the ball in Hemsby, a distance of approximately 15 miles. At 7.15 p.m., I rang my friend from a public call box close to the church to be told that he had failed in his attempt to borrow his father's car and would be travelling to the ball by motorcycle. His intention was to shuttle my partner and I from Ludham to Hemsby one at a time. The thought of my girlfriend dressed to kill in a long ballgown, riding pillion on a motorcycle was rather distressing. At 7.30 p.m., I rang again to be told that the motorcycle had failed to start and that my, by now ex-friend, was staying at home. Rescue came in the guise of Uncle Cecil Miller who kindly transported my girlfriend and I to Hemsby in his battered Morris car, not the most ideal form of transportation as the car was used primarily to deliver groceries to his customers and was filled with cardboard boxes, string and old newspapers. The front seat was also unattached to any part of the vehicle. Unfortunately as the lift was only one way, I still had to arrange transport back home again. Good relations between my girlfriend and I were re-established when we received an offer of a lift home from another friend, a motor mechanic whose partner also lived in Ludham. What he failed to say was that his transport was the garage pick-up truck and that, while there was room for my girlfriend in the cabin, I had to ride freezing to death on the back. As bad luck would have it, it rained!

Like cinema audiences, attendance at public dances declined when television established itself as an alternative attraction. As dance halls became primarily the province of the young, it was natural that dances would cater more for their tastes and that jiving would become tolerated. In 1958 the craze was for the cha-cha, popularised by the Ted Heath Band, Eddie Calvert and instrumental hit records such as 'Tea for Two' 'Cha-Cha, Cha-Cha in the Rain', 'Trumpet Cha-Cha' and 'Never on a Sunday'. In 1958, I joined the long lines of under-thirties dancing the cha-cha in unison across the dance floor at the Floral Hall. In 1959 it was the turn of jazz. At university, after sufficient fortification in the student bar, I joined my friends at the Saturday night dance in the main hall of the Percy Gee building. The dance – billed as the cheapest in Leicester – attracted large numbers of local young ladies in search of a student companion. Inevitably perhaps, standards changed as dances became more youth focussed. In 1960, I regularly attended dances at the Mecca-owned Palais de Danse in Leicester dressed in corduroy trousers, sweater, sports jacket and suede shoes – in the early 1950s I would never have been admitted. In the bigger dance halls, rock 'n' roll and jive were mixed in with the more traditional waltz, foxtrot and quickstep. However, from the mid-1950s some dances were organised to cater just for jive or rock 'n' roll. The first ever jazz and jive session in Great Yarmouth took place in November 1955, organised by the Far East Prisoner of War Association. The first ever rock 'n' roll evening occurred at the Queen's Hotel on Tuesday 11 December 1956.

Gorleston swimming pool with the Floral Hall behind. In my late teens, many of my sixth-form friends and I were regulars at the Saturday dance in the Floral Hall. (Colin Tooke)

TEENAGERS QUEUED FOR ROCK 'N' ROLL SESSION

The Pink Room of the Queen's Hotel was filled by teenage couples doing the rock 'n' roll dance from the musical 'Rock around the Clock' on Tuesday evening when Yarmouth's first rock 'n' roll evening was organised by the Gorleston dancing teacher, Mr Douglas Hall. Posters advertising the session had the comment 'not for squares'. For nearly three hours 150 teenagers jived and rocked to the latest records of Elvis Presley, Bill Haley and other rock 'n' roll stars. To the exciting rhythm of current hits such as 'Rudy's Rock' and 'Rip it up' girls were thrown over their partners' shoulders and between their legs.

Yarmouth Mercury, 14 December 1956

Thereafter, regular rock 'n' roll sessions were held not only at the Queen's Hotel but also at other venues in Great Yarmouth, especially at the Goode's Hotel and the Yare Hotel Ballroom. Eventually, every Wednesday at the Goode's Hotel was Juke Box Jamboree Night, where pop fans could rock 'n' roll to amplified pop records, an early version of a disco. Although many of my friends were regular rock 'n' rollers, my dancing visits to Yarmouth were mainly restricted to dances at the Floral Hall. I had been banned from both the Queen's and Goode's Hotels by my father, who associated rock 'n' roll with Teddy Boys and Teddy Boys with indolence and violence. Being a typical teenager I often enjoyed ignoring his ban, although the consequences if he found out would be disastrous; being a sixth former and still at school I relied on my father for my weekly pocket money. By the time jazz clubs had been established locally I was nineteen, at university, in receipt of a student grant, independent and deemed able to look after myself.

In 1959 my craze was exclusively for jazz music, or rather dancing to jazz music. My newfound university friends were all jazz fanatics, many of them playing instruments in jazz bands. Every Friday evening I danced to a student jazz band in the basement of the Percy Gee building in an atmosphere heavy with smoke and dust. Every Sunday I joined my friends at Club 57, an afternoon jazz club in a dance school above Burton's near Leicester's central Clock Tower. There I danced away the afternoon, mostly with two student friends, Mavis and Jill, both of whom were excellent dancers. Mavis was a great exponent of skip jive, which, under her tuition, I quickly mastered. In Leicester's De Montfort Hall I was privileged to hear many jazz greats including Kid Ory, The Modern Jazz Quartet, Terry Lightfoot and his New Orleans Jazz Band, and The Temperance Seven. On vacation back in Norfolk, I was a regular stomper at the Yarmouth Jazz Club in the Penrice Arms on King Street and at the United Jazz Club in Caister. Of the Norfolk bands, the most

The Collegians jazz band. Trips on the river with a jazz band accompaniment became very popular in the late 1950s. (© Eastern Daily Press 2007)

The Clock Tower and shopping centre, Leicester, 1960. A dance studio on the top floor above Burton's tailoring was the venue for the popular Sunday afternoon Club 57, where students and other enthusiasts gathered together to listen, stomp and jive to traditional jazz music. (© Leicestershire County Record Office)

proficient were the Collegians and the Mustard City Stompers. My already inflated ego was given a massive boost when, in August 1960, a university friend, Bob Gordon Walker, appeared as clarinettist with an ODJB (Original Dixieland Jazz Band) tribute band, the Original Downtown Syncopators, at the Caister-based United Jazz Club. My obvious acquaintance with members of the band ensured that I was not without a dance partner for most of the evening. Indeed, while the band was playing I was delighted to notice that another of Bob's friends and myself were both continually surrounded by the best-looking females in the room and a couple of tall sullen-looking gentlemen, assuming that my familiar-looking pale faced companion was also a student at Leicester University. At the end of the evening my ego took a nosedive when I suddenly realised that my companion was in fact Billy Fury, who was starring in 'Meet the Beat' at Yarmouth's Britannia Pier at the time, and it was he and not me that was attracting the females. The sullen six-footers were undoubtedly his minders.

JAZZ

We are happy to announce that a Jazz Cellar has been obtained in the basement of the Percy Gee building. Regular live sessions were begun last summer term by the Entertainments Committee and were greeted with a great deal of enthusiasm. It is fortunate that this session the Chairman of Entertainments is also a jazz enthusiast. It is hoped that the Jazz Cellar may be able to invite jazz bands from other universities, and for this reason alone, close cooperation between the Jazz Committee and the Entertainments Committee will be advantageous. A basic minimum of facilities exists; it is up to us to build on them.

Ripple, Leicester University, 9 October 1959

7

Music, Music, Music

MAKING MUSIC

'Music! Music! Music!', Teresa Brewer, 1950

It was during the 1950s that I discovered music. Perhaps discovered is the wrong word as, if anything, it was music that discovered me. Undoubtedly, it was peer pressure and teenage fashion combined with the emotions of adolescence that caused me to become susceptible to various musical influences. The 1950s were also exciting musically, evolving gradually from the big band music, crooners and ballad singers that were so popular with all ages early in the decade, through to the emergence of young people's music – rock 'n' roll, jazz, skiffle and folk – at the end. As a result, my musical taste was eclectic although it was heavily influenced by the popular trends of the day. Classical music was not part of my teenage culture and it remained unexplored throughout most of my early years.

Despite the absence of portable transistor radios, Walkman, iPods, MP3 players and their like, music was heard everywhere and not just from a radio in the home. People sang, whistled and hummed as they went about their daily business, not isolated behind headphones attached to a 'music provider' as is common today. Music while you work was a national ethos and making music was a pastime. Mother hummed and sang as she did her household chores, usually as an accompaniment to the radio, and my father always whistled through his teeth to aid his concentration when working. When groups of people met together either for work or for pleasure – the gangs in the fields harvesting fruit or potatoes, the ladies bunching flowers at our small market garden, the Happy Rollers on an outing, drinkers in the Horse & Groom or the passengers on a coach trip – they often ended up singing. Song followed song without a break, usually popular tunes that were easily recognised and sung with gusto, many of which were sentimental favourites from wartime – 'Pack up your troubles in your old kit bag', 'Maybe it's because I'm a Londoner', 'The Lambeth Walk', 'When Irish eyes are smiling', 'Underneath the lamplight', 'There'll be blue birds over the white cliffs of Dover' to mention but a few. Men whistled. A few women whistled but mother never did as she regarded whistling as unladylike. In her eyes, women who whistled were common. For boys it was important to be able to whistle, consequently Tony and I spent many hours in the playground at primary school puffing our cheeks, pouting our lips and blowing hard to master this essential skill.

Good singers found their outlets in concert parties and choirs, or just sang for pleasure at home. In Rollesby, both the church and the chapel had competent choirs, although the heyday of St George's Church choir had long passed. In the 1950s, chapel congregations were much larger than those at St George's Church and, consequently, it had the more proficient of the two choirs. A delight at Christmas was the sound of carol singing when these choirs toured around the

Carol singing on the Market Plain, Christmas 1957. (© Eastern Daily Press, 2007)

village, their paths lit by torches and hand-held lanterns, and their singing supported by an accordion, concertina or hand-bells. At Yarmouth Grammar School, the best singers were quickly recruited into the school choir. Apart from a short period as a choirboy at St George's Church, I had neither the interest nor the ability for choral singing. My first and last performance in a choir outside of a church was in 1951 when the first form at Yarmouth Grammar School was nominated by the music master to sing during the interval at the school's annual Christmas dramatic production. The play, *Le Bourgeois Gentilhomme*, was performed entirely in French and the songs chosen for us to sing were traditional French folksongs. Why the play was performed in French was, and still is, a mystery as the audience, consisting mainly of parents and their friends, was as ignorant of French as me. Had it been otherwise, the spectacle of first form boys singing songs in a language that they did not understand in a broad Norfolk accent would have undoubtedly appeared more comic than cultural. As it was, Tim and I mimed throughout the performance in case our obvious lack of talent elicited a reprimand from the headmaster. On the other hand, my mother's family had a long tradition of singing. Grandfather Cole was blessed with a good tenor voice and once sang in a choir at the Royal Albert Hall, Uncle Arthur Cole sang songs to a banjo accompaniment for his concert party in Great Yarmouth and, when he was young, my cousin Francis sang in St Nicholas' Church choir.

Cousin Francis dressed in his choirboy's surplice. Many members of my family sang for personal enjoyment as well as to entertain others. (Author's Collection)

In 1949 my parents bought a piano, a shiny new black upright piano that they placed in a prime position against the wall of our front room. During the 1950s, most families considered a piano to be an essential possession, whether or not anyone in the house could play it. Many of my aunts and uncles owned pianos, mostly old upright pianos that were out of tune and hardly ever touched. Grandfather Miller owned a harmonium, a smaller version of a church organ complete with pipes and stops, which took up a disproportionate amount of space in the living room at Hall Cottages. Occasionally he was persuaded to play slow dirge-like hymns, which he sang at the top of his voice while pumping away at the pedals and adjusting the stops. The sound was terrific, impressive and fun. Mother was keen that I should learn to play the piano and, on my tenth birthday, arranged for me to have lessons from Miss Dyball, a music teacher from Martham.

Despite great patience on her part, the lessons were a failure as no matter how hard I tried I could make no sense of musical notation. I could not tell a crotchet from a quaver or my FACE from my EGBDF. Any tunes that I could play, I learnt by ear. Not that the tunes were those that I wanted to play. Miss Dyball's practice pieces were mainly old English folk songs, sea shanties and simple excerpts from classical compositions. After a few months of effort on her behalf, she deemed me un-teachable and the lessons ceased. Thereafter the piano served only as a hiding place for my mother's cigarettes, save for when we were visited at Christmas by Aunt Eve Miller from Kent. Aunt Eve was an excellent pianist who could sight read music and, as a consequence, was the only person in the family who regularly played our piano, providing music for singing and dancing at our annual Christmas party.

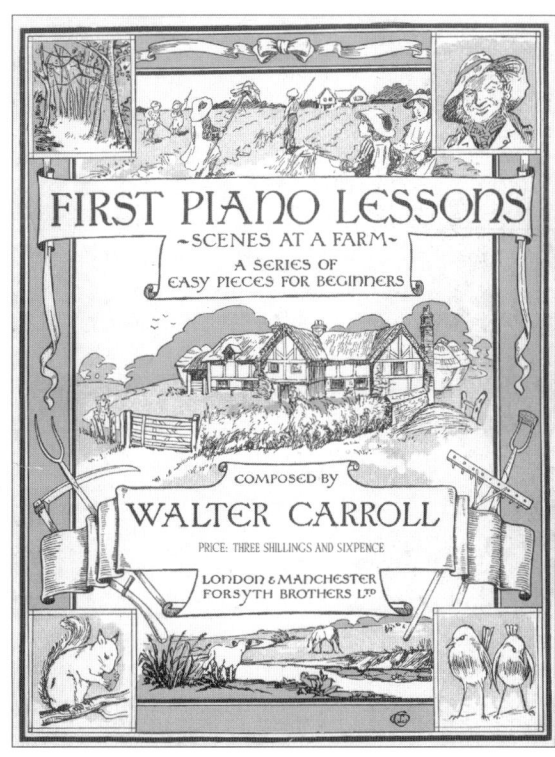

My interest in music was rekindled when I was given a harmonica as a fifteenth birthday present. Playing the harmonica proved not to be too difficult and very soon I was able to perform a number of recognisable popular tunes, much to my mother's delight. Uncle Billy Parnell was a talented harmonica player and regularly entertained at our parties. Under his tuition I learned techniques of breath control, vamping and how to use my hands to vary the sound. He also introduced me to the popular Hohner range of harmonicas and I was soon the proud owner of two Hohner models, a chromatic harmonica with a slide button and a banana-shaped Comet.

My interest was further heightened when I saw the Morton Fraser Harmonica Gang in a summer show at Great Yarmouth, a group of superb musicians who performed comedy routines, usually featuring a diminutive member of the group, while playing musical arrangements for the harmonica. I was not a Larry Adler fan as I considered his approach to music as being too serious and his playing action over exaggerated. At about the same time, Grandmother Miller gave me a rather battered ukulele-banjo and her collection of sheet music. Despite my inability to read music, I was able to teach myself how to play the ukulele as above the score were diagrams indicating the finger positions required for each chord. I eventually became quite competent at performing the songs from grandmother's sheet music which not only contained many jazzy numbers from the 1930s and '40s but also numerous George Formby hits including 'Chinese Laundry Blues', 'I'm Leaning on a Lamppost', 'Mister Wu', 'My Little Stick of Blackpool Rock', 'Ain't She Sweet' and 'When I'm Cleaning Windows'. Thereafter I was expected to do my musical bit at Christmas and at family parties. In 1957, armed with my harmonica and ukulele-banjo, I teamed up with a guitarist called Lenny Bridges to play skiffle music. Every weekend, accompanied by a tea chest bassist and washboard player, we made rhythmic noises in Lenny's front room. However, our efforts failed to gain universal appreciation and we were never asked to perform in public.

In 1958 I used all the money that I had earned during the summer vacation picking blackcurrants and beans and working in the harvest, to buy the instrument of the moment, an acoustic guitar. From then on I spent many long evenings in my bedroom with a Bert Weedon teach yourself guitar manual painfully learning finger positions and strumming out simple chord sequences. Within a few months I could play the chord sequences for a number of popular songs, which was not too difficult an accomplishment as most involved only four chord changes, C, A minor, F, and G7. All this was made easier by the fact that the fingering for the top four strings on the guitar was the same as that for the ukulele-banjo. I had merely to add fingering for the other two strings. By the time I began my university course, I considered myself to be a proficient musician. My arrival at Southmead House holding a ukulele-banjo, a guitar slung over my back and a harmonica in my pocket was greeted with great interest. My illusions were quickly shattered when I was introduced to another Southmead resident, a second-year mathematics student called Dave Cousins. Dave, a ginger-haired young man with a stubbly beard, turned out to be a guitarist of national standing and proficient in all styles of folk music, especially rhythm & blues. In comparison my guitar playing was simply naïve. Under Dave's guidance, together with long hours of practice, I not only successfully developed various techniques for playing the guitar – mainly finger-picking methods that included claw-hammer, slide and scratch – but was also introduced to the earthy music of numerous American folk legends such as Muddy Waters, Woodie Guthrie, Sonny Terry, Brownie Magee and Hudie Ledbetter (Leadbelly). By the end of my first year at university, along with Dave, I was a regular performer at the university's folk club and at the Red Cow, a public house in Leicester, where in an upstairs room an earnest but inebriated audience listened intently while seated on a strange collection of couches, chairs and canvas stools. Despite my conversion to rhythm &

Cast of the Leicester University Rag Revue, March 1960. I played my ukulele-banjo in a chaotic pit orchestra as well as performing a passable imitation of Cliff Richard. (Author's Collection)

blues, at Christmas, mother always requested that I should sing her favourite song, my rather innocuous version of 'Scarlet Ribbons'.

For the 1960 university rag revue, members of the university folk and jazz clubs decided to enter a comedy sketch entitled Crumbeat, allegedly a parody of BBC television's popular rock 'n' roll show, *Drumbeat*. To enhance the sound from our acoustic guitars, students from the physics department designed and made amplification equipment with pick-ups (small microphones), which they screwed precariously under the strings of our acoustic guitars. My contribution was as the character Husky Dusty Miller singing a rather risqué version of Cliff Richard's 'Voice in the Wilderness'. Unfortunately, the singing and playing were considered so good that nobody laughed and we were immediately inundated with requests for bookings.

Soon afterwards, with four other likeminded musicians – Rod, Russ, Trevor and Eric – I changed my musical direction away from folk music to become a founder member of Leicester University's first rock 'n' roll band, the Incas. For the next two

The Rag Revue.   *Poster advertising the Rag Ball.*

years I was able to enhance my student grant by playing bass guitar with the Incas, performing most weeks during the half-hour interval at the Saturday night dance in the Percy Gee building and as a support band at the various student balls held during the academic year. In order to finance our equipment, we applied for an unclaimed grant from the Students' Union that was intended to support a student-based operatic and dramatic society. To our surprise, our application was successful and the grant was awarded on the understanding that we would mount an operatic performance at the end of the academic year. With help from many friends, including a student from the English department who assumed the arduous roles of scriptwriter and producer, this daunting task was successfully accomplished. Under the guise of The Leicester University Musical and Operatic Society, the Incas delivered three performances of 'A Million Miles to the Moon', an original rock opera that developed the much exploited theme of the time – working class boy makes good, is led astray by fame and fortune and is rescued from destruction by his

The Incas, Leicester University's first rock 'n' roll band. Although it started as a joke, we all became serious rockers. (Author's Collection)

working class girlfriend. Despite our rather tongue-in-cheek approach to the event, the performances and original music received good reviews in the local press.

Buoyed with thoughts of becoming a pop star, I also joined a Leicester-based rock 'n' roll group, Johnny Angel and the Mystics, a local band consisting of four working class Leicester boys, Alan, Dougie, Dave and Baz, that played cover versions of current hit songs while performing rhythmic synchronised movements in the manner of Cliff Richard's backing group, the Shadows. On Saturday mornings and Wednesday evenings, practice sessions were held in the front room of Alan's terraced home, providing loud but free entertainment for Alan's mother in the kitchen and all the neighbours within 200 yards or more. Lead singer Dougie, a tough ex-Teddy Boy with a heart of gold, his thick Brylcreemed hair swept back in a DA style, gave performances under the stage name of Johnny Angel dressed in a gold lamé suit, white winkle-picker shoes and a red shirt with a frilly front. With the Mystics, I performed in numerous seedy Midlands' dance halls and various working men's clubs in Leicester, Coventry and Loughborough, often in a lunchtime variety show sandwiched between the bingo session, a talent competition for children and a stripper. Working with Dougie was always full of surprises. On one occasion, in the middle of a performance, Dougie leaped from the stage to confront a giant of a man who had unfortunately invited his girlfriend to dance. That evening we left hastily via the back door. After leaving university, my guitar mentor, Dave Cousins, embarked on a long career in music, establishing a popular professional group called the Strawbs and, in 1973, had a hit record with his song 'Part of the Union'. Despite my hopes and dreams, I eventually became a teacher!

More than any other period in my life, the 1950s and early '60s was the time when I made music myself, as well as listening to the music of others. Despite failing with the piano, I became sufficiently competent at playing three instruments (the harmonica, ukulele-banjo and guitar) to not only give me pleasure and satisfaction during my leisure hours but also to provide entertainment for friends, family and, occasionally, a paying public. My experience was not unique but was a common experience for many of my friends and relatives. Everybody sang, whistled or hummed at work and during their leisure time, mostly for pleasure but occasionally to entertain others. Most people aspired to play at least one instrument – harmonica, piano, accordion, violin or just paper and comb. Perhaps the songs of the day were simpler, more memorable or easier to play. Perhaps, without the modern plethora of technology for producing music, it was necessary to produce it oneself. Whatever the reason, Grandfather Cole sang for pleasure as well as in a choir, Uncle George Miller played a euphonium in a brass band and his wife, Aunt Eve, was a competent pianist. My Miller grandparents possessed not only a harmonium and two ukuleles but also an accordion and a concertina, which they played for their own personal enjoyment. Uncle Stanley Cole played the drums in a band at his Working Men's Club while Uncle Billy Parnell carried on his family's tradition of harmonica playing. More often than not, the choirs and dance bands that performed at Rollesby's village functions were made up from local singers and musicians. Without doubt, making music was an essential part of many people's leisure time during the 1950s.

LISTENING TO MUSIC

'Love is like a violin', Ken Dodd, 1960

Before the age of thirteen, I can't say that I made a deliberate effort to listen to music although, as a child, I was surrounded by music and song. At primary school, we listened and learnt to sing traditional British folksongs, usually from the BBC's weekday programmes for schools. I learnt the songs my family sung and listened with my parents to their choice of music on the radio. As a child, I preferred novelty songs and repeatedly sung family favourites. But at the age of thirteen, as my hormones kicked in and I developed emotional crushes on unobtainable females, I saw music in a different light. As I fantasised over Elizabeth, Dorothy and Linda, my knees weakened every time I heard Frankie Laine's version of the evocative song,

'Answer Me'. I even imaged myself singing it to them in a bid for their affections. Luckily, I never found the courage. Thereafter, as my tastes changed from children's songs to popular as well as romantic music, I forsook former favourites like 'I Taut I Taw a Puddy Tat', 'How Much is that Doggie in the Window?' and 'Rudolph the Red-Nosed Reindeer', to listen alone to my own choice of programmes on the radio in my bedroom. I listened every Sunday to *Two Way Family Favourites* in the hope of hearing pop songs of the day, followed by *Billy Cotton's Band Show* with the delightful Alma Cogan, another of my fantasies. I even endured Saturday morning's *Children's Favourites*, with Uncle Mac (Derek McCulloch) and the frequently played 'Runaway Train', 'Sparky's Magic Piano', 'The Teddy Bears' Picnic' and 'Three Billy Goats Gruff', for an occasional popular adult tune. But by the mid-1950s, my programmes of choice were those broadcast by Radio Luxembourg, programmes peddling music for the young, exciting music, revolutionary music and not for the old. Imagine my horror when mother announced that she had just heard a lovely song from a very nice young man – 'Singing the Blues' by Tommy Steele. I liked it too! Parents were meant to be old and square, and satisfied with their big band music, not aficionados of rock 'n' roll. In the late 1950s, under pressure from ITV and Radio Luxembourg, programmes on BBC's television and radio began to include music for the young. I kept abreast with the latest popular music through BBC television's *6-5 Special*, *Drumbeat* and *Juke Box Jury*, BBC radio's *Pick of the Pops* with Alan Dell and David Jacobs, and Brian Matthews' *Saturday Club*, not forgetting the obligatory top 20 on Luxembourg.

More often than not listening to music in the late 1950s meant listening to gramophone records. Encouraged by youth-focussed magazines such as the *New Musical Express*, young people with increasingly more money in their pockets were able to buy regular purchases from local music shops, mainly the latest pop music on unbreakable 7in 45rpm records. Additionally, the development of affordable small portable record players, particularly the Dansette Junior and Senior, enabled teenagers to listen to records in their bedrooms away from their parents and to play music for dancing at parties. Before the mid-1950s, record players were big, bulky and much too expensive for most people to own. My Miller grandparents possessed a pre-war wind-up gramophone for playing their collection of 78rpm discs, mostly scratchy and often-cracked recordings of 1930s dance music. In the early 1950s, Uncle Billy Parnell bought a radiogram, a combined radio and gramophone contained in a large walnut cabinet, which he placed under the window of his living room. For entertainment, he spent many hours listening to his collection of Bing Crosby, Frank Sinatra and Doris Day records. Richard was the first of my friends to own a modern portable electric record player – a red leatherette three-speed Dansette Senior with an auto-changer for playing stacked records one after the other. We spent many hours in the kitchen of his home listening to his record collection that consisted mainly of light orchestral pieces such as 'The Coronation Scott' and 'The Westminster Waltz'. In 1956 our tastes were changed completely when he bought a long play record entitled *Elvis Presley* – a groundbreaking record that contained most of Elvis' early hits including 'Heartbreak Hotel', 'Blue Suede Shoes', 'I got a Woman', 'Money Honey' and 'Lawdy Miss Clawdy'. We spent many hours playing this record time after time and providing out-of-tune vocal accompaniments to all of the tracks.

In 1957 I bought my first record player, a beige and red Dansette Junior single play model with three speeds to accommodate 78, 45 and 33rpm records, which I acquired second-hand for £2. This was a bargain, as in 1957 a new Dansette record player was unaffordable at 14 guineas and an HMV 4-speed automatic radiogram totally beyond my capabilities at 56 guineas. The plastic playing arm contained a rotating cartridge with two needles, one for the old-fashioned and easily damaged 78rpm shellac records and the other for the newer and more robust vinyl 45rpm singles, EPs, and 33rpm LPs. From then on, I spent most Saturday mornings with my school friends evaluating possible record purchases from the current Top Twenty in six small listening booths at Wolsey & Wolsey's electrical shop on King Street in Great Yarmouth. Despite the cost involved – a 45rpm single retailed at 6s 11d, a relatively large sum in those days – I quickly amassed a comprehensive collection of popular music records, mainly 45s together with two EPs featuring Mr Acker Bilk & his Paramount Jazz Band and Billy May & his Orchestra, and one LP of Chris Barber in Concert. When I eventually left home bound for Leicester, I gave the record player to my mother and, under the misguided impression that popular music was non-U for university students, divided my pop music collection between my mother and my cousin Stephanie. My jazz records were packed in my trunk and accompanied me to college.

I was also fascinated by jukeboxes, large gaudy illuminated cabinets that, for a charge of 6d placed in a slot, played a selected record from a choice of one hundred or more 45rpm discs. I first encountered a jukebox at the Queens Hotel at the seaside end of Regent Road in Great Yarmouth. The hotel had become an informal coastal base for off-duty American servicemen from the many US airfields located in East Anglia. Consequently the public bar at the Queens Hotel had been adapted to provide for the needs of its American visitors, including the provision of two jukeboxes, one at each end of the bar with sufficient free space for jiving. Despite the obvious hostility that existed between US servicemen and the local Norfolk youth, I frequently visited the Queens not only to buy the cheap black-market American cigarettes on offer from the servicemen but also to listen to the latest recordings played on the jukeboxes, many of which were American imports. By 1960, most of the amusement arcades along Marine Parade had also added jukeboxes to their other moneymaking attractions. I spent many hours in the summer of 1960 leaning against a jukebox in an amusement arcade next to the Hippodrome Circus on Great Yarmouth's seafront among a large gang of like-minded teenagers, many of whom jived to the music, much to the annoyance of the arcade owner. I can clearly recollect repeated plays of one particular hit record, Johnny Kidd & the Pirates' version of 'Shakin' All Over', which was accompanied vocally by most of the attendant teenagers, many of whom were providing air guitar impressions during the guitar solos. Old, worn or out-of-date discs were regularly replaced by the jukebox owners and offered for sale cheaply to local youngsters. Plastic inserts were required for all these discs as, in order to fit the jukebox's playing mechanism, their centres had been removed. Despite this, the discs were in great demand owing to the high

Local musicians Johnny Austin, Eddie Bates and Billy Crowe. In the 1950s, most people aspired to play at least one musical instrument. Accordions were popular as they were easily transportable and loud enough to play music for dancing. (Eddie Bates)

cost of new shop-bought recordings. Many in my own record collection were ex-jukebox 45s.

Other than that played on a record player, the radio or television, music in the 1950s was mainly live music, performed by individuals, choirs, groups, orchestras and bands either for dancing or as a concert. My preference was for music that I could dance to. Dancing was my pleasure and I was good at it no matter whether modern ballroom or jive and, besides, it provided me with the means for meeting females. I enjoyed Eddie Bates' band at a village hop, the big bands at the Floral Hall and the jazz groups at Club 57 because they provided music for dancing rather than music just for listening to. I even considered rock 'n' roll to be first and foremost dance music. Nevertheless, I could sing, hum, whistle and play most of the current rock 'n' roll tunes. Although I enjoyed all forms of music, sitting and listening for a long period of time was not my style, no matter whether the concert was folk, choral, mainstream or classical. I enjoyed the brass bands that played at the local village fêtes or in the bandstand on Great Yarmouth's St George's Park, but after ten minutes or so I had had enough. I endured Neville Bishops' orchestra at the Marina, an open-air music auditorium on Great Yarmouth's seafront, because of the competitions that were also part of the entertainment. I wriggled in my seat while listening to the sopranos and tenors in the summer season's variety shows. I enjoyed popular music on my radio and record player but preferred playing and dancing to listening to live music.

During my teens I only ever attended one classical music concert. Despite music lessons every week at grammar school, in which *Peter and the Wolf* featured on more occasions than I care to recall, and short excerpts at morning assembly, I hardly ever listened to classical music pieces. My parents preferred their big band music and my friends the popular music of the day. When Tony began listening to classical music records, we thought that he had become strange and treated him accordingly. My first and only experience of a classical concert was when the upper school of Yarmouth Grammar School was invited to join the audience at a lunchtime concert of music played by the BBC Concert Orchestra to be broadcast live from Yarmouth's Town Hall. Along with one hundred or more senior boys, Tim and I sat uncomfortably on the hard Town Hall chairs, sweltering in the midday heat listening in awe to the wall of sound emanating from the fifty or so musicians on the stage. As instructed, when the music stopped Tim and I applauded enthusiastically only to discover that we were the only ones showing such appreciation. As we were unfamiliar with the piece, how were we to know that a pause existed in between its two parts? Not only was our embarrassment patently obvious to the Headmaster, with the inevitable repercussions, but also to the thousands of people listening on the radio. The conductor was clearly not amused although many members of the orchestra smiled.

I enjoyed listening to the songs at the folk clubs, primarily because it enabled me to extend my own repertoire. Being unable to read music, I could only learn new songs and improve my playing techniques by watching and listening to other performers. My only reservation was that too many of the singers were far too serious about folk music. Some took great delight in discovering and performing

The Great Pretender	The Platters
Love is Strange	Mickey & Sylvia
Freight Train	Chas McDevitt & Nancy Whiskey
All Shook Up	Elvis Presley
Lucille	Little Richard
Bye Bye Love	The Everly Brothers
Last Train to San Fernando	Johnny Duncan
Wake up Little Susie	The Everly Brothers
Great Balls of Fire	Jerry Lee Lewis
Diana	Paul Anka
Peggy Sue	Buddy Holly & The Crickets
Oh Boy	The Crickets
At the Hop	Danny & The Juniors
Sweet Little Sixteen	Chuck Berry
All I have to do is Dream/Caludette	The Everly Brothers
Purple People Eater	Sheb Wooley
Just an Old Fashioned Girl	Eartha Kitt
Rave On	Buddy Holly & The Crickets
Endless Sleep	Marty Wilde
When	The Kalin Twins
Think it Over	The Crickets
Poor Little Fool	Ricky Nelson
Bird Dog	The Everly Brothers
Move It	Cliff Richard & The Shadows
Western Movies	The Olympics
Tom Dooley	Lonnie Donegan
It's Only Make Believe	Conway Twitty
Does Your Chewing Gum Lose Its Flavour	Lonnie Donegan
It Doesn't Matter Any More	Buddy Holly & The Crickets
Donna	Marty Wilde
C'mon Eveybody	Eddie Cochrane
A Teenager in Love	Craig Douglas
Here Comes Summer	Jerry Keller
The Battle of New Orleans	Lonnie Donegan
Till I Kissed You	The Everly Brothers
Sea of Love	Marty Wilde

Singles from my record collection, 1957–9.

obscure country songs or fishermen's shanties, often unmemorable dirges about shipwrecks and hangings, which they sang unaccompanied with their eyes closed and a finger in one ear. I had a feeling for songs that had a rhythm and guitar music that had some substance. Consequently, my preferences veered towards American rhythm & blues that told tales about railways, triumph over adversity and San Francisco Bay. Perhaps I should have been born Bob Dylan.

8

Sporting Opportunities

SPORTS FACILITIES

'Its all in the game', Tommy Edwards, 1958

An essential facility for sport in the villages was a council-owned recreation field. Because of the war, many had become poorly maintained but, by the early 1950s, they were gradually being restored for use. Rollesby was fortunate in that it had a designated King George V Memorial Playing Field, one of nearly 500 recreation fields created throughout the country after the death of King George in 1936 and financed by a foundation set up to commemorate his reign. As was often the case, the playing field was established on land acquired next to the village school and during the day doubled as a sports field for the school children. Other Flegg villages were not so lucky and did not have a designated playing field. Their sporting activities usually took place on meadowland or common within the village or in the parkland of the local Hall by permission of the resident landowner. I frequently played football and cricket matches on fields that had just been cleared of cattle, with the inevitable hazards of muddy patches and cowpats. Cricket squares were normally roped off and carefully maintained, but the outfields on working meadows and parkland were left to fend for themselves. While the grass was usually clipped short by grazing animals, odd islands of nettles and thistles remained adding an interesting obstacle to play in football and cricket matches. Changing rooms were a luxury, showers and wash rooms a rarity. Players frequently changed in the team's coach if they came in one, a car if they had one or, occasionally, a hut or cattle shed, if there was one. Otherwise teams arrived already dressed for the game or changed their clothes in the open air, much to the amusement of any female spectators or curious children.

Like village halls, the late 1940s and early '50s witnessed a government-sponsored drive to establish recreation fields in rural communities. In 1953, nearby Filby village financed the purchase of a playing field with a grant from the Playing Fields Association, while Burgh Castle used funds from its Welcome Home Committee, an organisation originally set up to benefit men returning from war service with the armed forces. In Martham, despite some initial resistance, money raised by the efforts of the villagers together with a grant from the Norfolk Education Committee was used to create a large sports field on the Rollesby Road near to Martham Station. A large modern pavilion was added and opened in May 1959.

PLAYING FIELD MEETING

A public meeting sponsored by the Parish Council was held in the Institute when the County Education Officer (Mrs Lewis) described the procedure to be adopted should the meeting decide to go forward with a scheme to provide a Playing Field for the village. Mr A.A. Francis presided. It was generally agreed that there is a real need for a Playing Field but the will to provide one did not appear to be present. In the discussion, Mr W.R. Chapman said that what was required was somebody to loan the village a meadow to provide for football and cricket. He drew attention to the state of the tennis courts and bowling greens at the Institute which had been in disuse since the beginning of the war. Mr W.F. Temple said he could not see how a Playing Field could be acquired without the full cooperation of all the village. He pointed out that the one single meadow was now used for as many as three football matches on a Saturday and had also to provide a cricket pitch in the summer. The greatest difficulty appeared to be the problem of enlisting the cooperation of the youths who found the thrills of speedway and other organised professional sports more satisfying than the efforts required to improve the amenities of their own village.
'Village news, Martham', *Yarmouth Mercury*, 27 May 1949

King George V Memorial Playing Field was and still is located on the main road through Rollesby, next to the village primary school. In the 1950s this green area provided a playing surface for Rollesby's football and cricket teams, as well as a venue for the church fête, school sports day and the village bonfire celebrations. In one corner was a popular children's play area consisting of three swings, a seesaw and a sand pit. In the furthest corners away from the Main Road were two toilets; a facility for the men consisting of a square enclosure made from corrugated iron sheets and a lockable shed with a chemical toilet for the women. Adjacent to the school, the small green wooden hut served as a changing room for visiting cricket and football teams as well as a meeting place for the Women's Club. The veranda attached to the hut, erected to celebrate the Coronation of Queen Elizabeth II, provided a dry all-year-round meeting place for Rollesby's youth. In the winter, goalposts were permanently erected on the playing field and were not only used for Saturday matches by Rollesby's football team but also during the remainder of the week by scores of village boys developing their soccer skills. By the end of the season the pitch, particularly by the goal area, was extremely worn and denuded of grass. Unfortunately, in the summer the same area was used by the cricket team for its matches. The playing square was, therefore, particularly rough giving a definite advantage to a team with good bowlers and placing the batsmen at risk of serious injury. Although the grass on the playing square was kept short by the cricket club's small motor mower, without the benefit of gang-mowers the outfield became thick with grass despite occasional assistance from a number of tethered goats. Inevitably scores in cricket matches were usually low and games were often finished by teatime. In 1956 a concrete practice strip was added close to the main entrance to provide a facility for net practice. As the crease area and bowler's run up were left as grass, frequent use of the concrete strip resulted in these areas being hollowed out over time. By the end of the season, batsmen were taking guard at a crease often six inches below the concrete practice playing surface, tempting the bowlers to indulge in exhibitions of aggressive bodyline bowling.

Although King George's Playing Field was a popular meeting place for children and teenagers (to play hotly contested games of football and cricket, to talk, to make friends and to discuss issues of importance to young people), for sports-mad country children it was not an essential facility. Meadows, village greens, commons and private gardens provided ample space for playing games. Except for the major highways, even the minor roads were relatively safe to use. I spent many hours either by myself or with my friends practicing catching a tennis ball by bouncing it against a convenient wall, dribbling a football along Martham Road or developing my penalty shooting skills against our outside toilet door. Opposite to our house on Martham Road was a small wooden garage with a grassed area in front which proved to be an ideal location for Tony and me to play long games of football and cricket. In the summer, we spent many hours in the meadows adjoining Martham Road playing football with our jumpers laid out as the goalposts, and cricket with twigs from the hedgerows as wickets. At harvest time, the farm workers of Hall Farm often finished the day by playing games of football in the meadow near to Martham Road, using their pitchforks as goalposts. My father and I frequently joined them, as did most of the other young men and children in the neighbourhood. It was not uncommon to see these athletic young adults in their working overalls and hobnail boots playing quality games of soccer while being pursued by hoards of yelling children. Great Yarmouth on the other hand was blessed with many more council-owned recreation fields, parks and children's playgrounds, although emergent footballers still made use of any convenient space for their games – open areas behind houses, undeveloped bomb sites, cul-de-sacs and alleyways as well as the beach and the sand dunes. I often played ball games in an alleyway next to Grandma Cole's house, disturbed only by the occasional herd of cattle on their way to the abattoir behind.

PLAYING SPORT

'Great Balls of Fire', Jerry Lee Lewis, 1957

Organised outdoor sport in the Flegg villages mainly consisted of football and cricket. Every village had well-supported football and cricket teams, and matches between villages were keenly contested, particularly those between neighbouring villages. Most village boys treated their football and cricket team members as local heroes and aspired to become members themselves in due course – at least I did. I was lucky that my father was a footballer of some distinction and Uncle Cecil Miller was an enthusiastic cricketer. Under their tuition, I eventually progressed to play regularly for Rollesby's football and cricket teams.

My father's football skills were recognised quite early and, as a consequence, at the age of ten he was persuaded to transfer from Rollesby to Martham School where the football training was of a higher quality. At thirteen he became captain of a successful East Flegg Boys team, and eventually joined Gorleston Juniors where he played in a side that included the young Albert 'Sailor' Brown, probably the most famous footballer from this region. While living in Birmingham, he won medals playing for Hearts Old Boys in the West Midlands League and was assessed by scouts from Aston Villa with a view to playing professionally. Unfortunately, the war interrupted his progress and by the time he was demobbed in 1947, he was too old for anything other than local football. During his army service he represented his regiment, playing with and against many well-known professional footballers. He always contended that playing football may have saved his life because after a serious injury to his knee ligaments during a training match he spent six months in hospital, while his regiment embarked for North Africa where it sustained heavy casualties. On his return from army service he played one season for Yarmouth Town Reserves before joining Rollesby's village football team. Perhaps the games were more physical then, as my only memory of his time with the 'Bloaters' was of watching from the main stand at the Wellesley ground as he was carried off to hospital on a stretcher to receive six stitches in a gash over one eye. Mother was naturally worried but I was immensely proud of his battle scars. He eventually hung up his football boots in 1956 on reaching the age of forty, the time when, according to mother, men should stop playing sport and settle down to impending old age. For the rest of the decade he spent many Saturday afternoons acting as a linesman at home matches, running up and down the touchline waving a dirty handkerchief in place of a linesman's flag.

Luckily for my father, the early 1950s were not only the heyday of village football but also the best years of Rollesby Football Club. In 1950, Rollesby FC was competing in Division 2 of the Great Yarmouth & District Football League – a league established in 1907 to provide a competitive structure for junior soccer in Great Yarmouth and consisting mainly of town-based factory and office teams together with sides from neighbouring Broadland villages within a 15-mile radius. Rollesby's home pitch was at King George's Playing Field, where the hut provided relatively comfortable changing facilities. Playing normally in a strip of white shirts and black shorts with black and white hooped socks, Rollesby FC soon acquired the nickname of 'The Lillywhites'. Like most rural teams in the early 1950s, players and spectators were mainly drawn from the village. As a result, the possibility of success depended very much upon the talent available in the immediate locality. In the early 1950s, Rollesby village boasted a number of gifted football players and, with their inclusion in the village team, the football club embarked on a decade of unrepeated success. Those few members of the team drawn from outside the village were often taunted as 'tourists' by opposition spectators and accused of medal hunting. Mother loved watching football and every Saturday she joined the fifty or more exceedingly vocal supporters standing along the touchline at a match no matter where the team was playing and whether or not it was raining. The home team's supporters usually stood on one side of the pitch and the away team's supporters on the other, as their enthusiasm for events on the pitch frequently boiled over into conflict off the pitch, especially in derby or cup matches between neighbouring villages. Football and

Rollesby Football Club, Wiltshire Cup finalists, 1959. Most village teams in the 1950s consisted mainly of local residents. (Sheila Allen)

cricket matches between Martham and Rollesby were always hard fought and often resulted in bloody confrontations both on and off the field.

SPECTATORS INVADE PITCH

Reedham's visit to Potter Heigham last Saturday in the Wiltshire Cup ended unfortunately when, with Reedham leading 3–2 and only one minute left to play, the referee abandoned the game when spectators invaded the pitch and refused to leave. It had been an even game. Reedham's goals were scored by C. Mace (2) and L. Howard.

'Village News, Reedham', *Yarmouth Mercury*, 8 February 1952

Rollesby Football Club's greatest achievements undoubtedly occurred during the early 1950s, and were made all the more special by the fact that the management and players of both the first and reserve teams were mostly village residents, drawn from a total population of no more than 500 people. In 1952, Rollesby's first team became Division 2 champions, winners of the Bradfield Cup and runners-up to

Halvergate in the Yarmouth League Cup. Subsequently, the club completed a successful decade by ending as runners-up in 1959 to Gorleston United in the prestigious Wiltshire Cup, allegedly the second oldest continuously contested competition in English amateur football. The second team also achieved honours by winning the Flegg Reserve Team Cup on two successive occasions and becoming the first winners of the Burgess Cup in 1954.

FOOTBALL CLUB DINNER

Eighty members and supporters of Rollesby Football Club were present at the club's annual dinner at the Bridge Hotel, Potter Heigham on Saturday when Mr W.R. Masterson, chairman of the Norfolk County F.A. presented the Burgess Cup to the captain of Rollesby Reserves, Mr E. Evans. The team beat Bradwell in the final. Mr P. Nockolds, hon. sec of the Yarmouth & District League congratulated Rollesby on being the first team to win the cup. The club's president, Mr H. Youngs, presided. The members of the cup winning team were M. Rose, C. Ransome, R. Miller, R. Attew, E. Evans, S. Evans, J. Bates, B. Harrison, R. Irwin, E. Catchpole, S. Barber and R. Smith.

'Village news, Rollesby', *Yarmouth Mercury*, 21 May 1954

Nevertheless, the pinnacle of Rollesby Football Club's success came during the 1950/1 and 1951/2 seasons when the first team reached consecutive finals of the

Rollesby Football Team, 1950. Back row: my father, Clifford Tooke, Steve Barber, Maurice Rose, Ricky Ribbons, Ozzie Lambert. Front row: Bobby Smith, Bobby Catchpole, Johnny Smith, Harold Rose, Johnny Harrison. (Author's Collection)

countywide Norfolk Primary Cup, unfortunately losing in both matches 5–2 to Costessey in 1951 and 2–1 to Hevingham in 1952. Both games were played at Carrow Road, home of Norwich City Football Club, and as my father took part in each, mother and I were among the 200 or more vociferous villagers supporting the valiant but vain efforts of our team to bring the cup home to Rollesby. My clearest memories, however, are not of the finals but of the 1952 semi-final against Edgefield on a windswept north Norfolk pitch. One hundred and fifty or more villagers made the 1½-hour journey from Rollesby, the majority packed into three coaches provided by Bensley's of Martham. Everybody displayed some token of support for the team, black and white rosettes and scarves, or placards urging 'Up the Lillywhites'. My contribution was a very noisy rattle. As I remember, the game was so exciting that even the younger supporters watched with the adults, me included, desisting from our own kick-about on the sidelines. I was particularly enthralled as my father played an important part in the victory and was clearly man-of-the-match. The journey home was slow, noisy and involved many refreshment stops at wayside public houses.

ROLLESBY AGAIN IN THE PRIMARY CUP FINAL

Rollesby, leaders of Division 2 of the Yarmouth & District League, reached the final of the Norfolk Primary Cup for the second successive season on Saturday when they beat Edgefield 4–1 at Holt. Rollesby's success means that the League will have been represented in three consecutive Primary Cup Finals. Dyson's were beaten 2–0 by St Faiths two seasons ago. Last season Rollesby lost 5–2 to Costessey Sports Club. Their semi-final win on Saturday was as decisive as the score suggests. A goal ahead through right-winger Symonds within five minutes of the start, Rollesby increased their lead in the 20th minute when R. Miller scored with a 40-yard drive. Symonds made it 3–0 before the interval when a free kick by Miller hit the bar and S. Barber added a fourth in the second half after a left-wing run. Edgefield's goal came near the end from a rebound off the bar. Rollesby, who were well supported, were the more polished and consistent side and well deserved the right to meet the winners of tomorrow's semi-final between Hevingham and North Creake.

Yarmouth Mercury, 28 March 1952

Although, through endless hours of practice and much useful advice from my father, I had developed some ability at football, my soccer experiences can only be described as too little and too late. At ten years of age, I was selected for Rollesby primary school's football team the year after it had won all the local inter-primary school competitions. I joined Rollesby Reserves in 1955 as their Burgess Cup winning side reached football retirement age leaving the team in drastic need of rebuilding. I eventually graduated to the first team in 1957 as relegation from Division 1 threatened. At Yarmouth Grammar, I played senior football for South House and was a regular member of the school first team during my sixth form years. Despite this success, I only accidentally discovered that I had been awarded my coveted football colours the year after I had left school.

In cricket I was more fortunate. For Rollesby Cricket Club, the late 1950s was a successful period in its playing history and, in my late teens, it provided an opportunity for me to experience the joy of winning rather than the frustration of losing. Although my father was a fast bowler of some ability, it was my Uncle Cecil Miller, a cricket fanatic, who encouraged my interest in the game. Rollesby Cricket Club was his summer passion and he served as secretary of the club for over fifty years following its foundation in 1930. As unofficial groundsman, he spent most summer evenings tending to the pitch, mowing, rolling and marking the wicket and

Uncle Cecil Miller receiving a clock in recognition of his twenty-five years service to Rollesby Cricket Club. Many village clubs and societies thrived due to the dedication and hard work of a few individuals within the community. (Stephanie and Barry Gallant)

boundaries, or practicing with the team in the nets. He was never happier than when he was tinkering with the motor mower, delivering the team selection cards or just talking cricket to another enthusiast. As a player he was an all-rounder – a middle order batsman and a specialist spin bowler. When he bowled, his style was mesmeric and often produced a dramatic turnaround in fortunes during games that were almost lost. As he was well over 6ft tall his bowling pace was very slow with an extremely high trajectory. Opposition batsmen frequently described the ball as 'coming down with snow on it.' His ability to make the ball spin both ways with a variable bounce earned him the nickname 'Crafty Miller' and a deserved reputation as a wicket taker. His passion was supported by his wife, Aunt Doris Miller, who was almost as fanatical about cricket herself. Most Saturday and Sunday mornings, she spent at least two hours preparing teas for afternoon home matches, usually boiled egg, cucumber or tomato sandwiches, buns and cakes. In the afternoon she was team scorer, sitting at a trestle table officiating while nervously chain-smoking. At thirteen years of age, my initial function for the club was to tend the scoreboard, which leaned precariously against the scorer's table. Occasionally, I was asked by Aunt Doris to score when the opposition had nobody available to tend their scorebook. Sometimes I was asked to play when our team arrived at a game short of a player. At sixteen I became a regular playing member.

CRICKET CLUB SECRETARY FOR 25 YEARS

At a dinner to celebrate the 25th anniversary of Rollesby Cricket Club held at Matthes restaurant on Saturday, Mr C.A. Miller, the secretary of the club since its formation, was presented with a clock on behalf of the club and supporters. The presentation was made by Mr B. Harrison (assistant secretary) and a tribute to Mr Miller's long service was paid by Mr M. Rose (captain). Mr F. Moore (club chairman) presided and among those present were Col I.B.H. Benn and Capt P.I.H. Benn. On view were the Yarmouth & District 20-over Cup and the Flegg & District 20-over Cup won by the club last season.

'Village news, Rollesby', *Yarmouth Mercury*, 4 November 1955

Like many other village sides, Rollesby Cricket Club shared its facilities with the football club, both using King George's Playing Field as their home base. In the 1940s and '50s, there was no overlap between the cricket and football seasons. When one season ended the other began, even in the professional game, enabling players to participate in both sports and the same ground to be used by both clubs. Unfortunately for the cricket club, Rollesby's recreation field was not large enough for a designated cricket square to be kept separate from the football pitch. In the winter the footballers played over the area that became the cricket wicket in the summer. Consequently, despite frantic early season efforts with cutter and roller, it was never possible to prepare a perfect playing surface for the summer. Rollesby's solution was to cover the wicket with coconut matting held down tight by a number of iron tent pegs. The result was a fairly slow and predictable wicket unless the bowler managed to hit one of the pegs, when the ball would then deviate in an erratic manner, occasionally onto the stumps. Many other village clubs suffered similarly from sharing a pitch with football and had their own solutions, usually the installation of a single concrete wicket. The municipal grounds of Great Yarmouth, such as the Beaconsfield (adjacent to the Grammar School), were a different matter as they were large enough to have cricket squares separate from football pitches and were attended by specialist groundsmen.

In 1958, a permanent solution for Rollesby was found when the resident of the New Rollesby Hall, Captain Patrick Benn, donated a portion of his surrounding parkland as a designated cricket ground to be used in perpetuity by the cricket club. After a great effort by club members, the rough parkland, formerly used for grazing cattle, was fenced, levelled and a new grass playing square established. The first matches were played at the new ground in the summer of 1959. Without unlimited funds or resources, initiative was required to solve many initial problems. A second-hand chalet was purchased from a holiday camp in Hemsby to be used as a pavilion and was filled with a motley collection of old chairs and sofas begged or borrowed from village residents. An overhead cable provided the electricity and a single standpipe supplied all the water needed for tea, washing and watering the pitch.

The author playing with a dog while waiting to bat, 1957. (Author's Collection)

To help create a perfect outfield, a set of gang-mowers was attached to a battered old car which was left permanently unlocked, filled with petrol and with the ignition keys left inside. As a result, many young people learned to drive in the old car while unwittingly mowing the outfield at the same time. Next to the new ground, an old sandpit was home to ten or more large pigs. Fielders retrieving balls hit into the sandpit did so with a great deal of trepidation.

The majority of cricket players were again village residents, drawn from all age groups and every level of village society. A few, especially those who had been educated at public school, came dressed in well-pressed whites, boots, striped blazers and hooped caps, with their personal kit contained in a long thin leather bag and their trousers held up by an old school tie instead of a belt. The remainder were mainly agricultural and other workers who wore well-worn whites, whitened plimsolls, or boots if they could afford them, and shared a varied collection of bats, pads and gloves contained in the club's large leather cricket bag. For those who learned their cricket on the rough pitches of the immediate post-war period, style

Members of Rollesby Cricket Club celebrating a win in the 1955 Coronation Cup. This successful side consisted mainly of players living in the village. Uncle Cecil Miller stands second from the left. (Richard Tacon)

was not an issue. Like my father, many of Rollesby's batsmen were drawn from the 'agricultural' school of cricket where the intention was to hit the ball as hard as possible, hopefully out of the ground, while trying to avoid being hurt due to the regular unpredictable bounce. The most perfect exponent of this batting style was Lenny Hodds, a thick-set, mild-mannered, curly-haired and exceptionally strong young man with an excellent eye for a ball, who, despite having only two basic shots – an impenetrable forward defensive block and a free flowing cross bat drive (some called it a swipe) – regularly performed miracles on erratic pitches. In 1952, Lenny scored Rollesby's first post-war century in the Beck Cricket League, when he blasted 115 not out in record time against a battered Upton village side.

Throughout the 1950s, Rollesby played in the Beck Cricket League, a Saturday league established by George Beck in 1932 for village sides from the Broadland Fleggs that also included teams from Fleggburgh, Filby, Freethorpe, Ormesby, Halvergate, Hemsby & Winterton, Martham, Runham and Upton. On Sunday, a second team played in the Great Yarmouth Weekend League and, as well as midweek friendly games, a representative side competed in various knock-out competitions including the Flegg & District Beck 20-over Cup, the Loveday Cup and the Yarmouth & District Coronation Cup. Success for Rollesby in the late 1950s included becoming the first village side to win both the Beck and Coronation 20-over Cups in the same season (1955), Beck League Champions (1957) and winners of the Great Yarmouth Weekend League for five consecutive years (1956–60). With increasing car ownership, players of both cricket and football were able to travel further to participate in games. Consequently, by the 1960s clubs began to lose their village identities, resulting in a reduction in local support. Rollesby and Martham Cricket Clubs still thrive, owing mainly to their excellent playing facilities. Many other Flegg village teams have long been consigned to the dustbin of sporting history. Rollesby Football Club is no longer in existence and, inevitably, local players have become 'tourists' in other village soccer teams.

Apart from football and cricket, and bowls at the Horse & Groom, there were no other competitive outdoor sporting activities available in the village for Rollesby people. Not that things were any better in the neighbouring villages or, indeed, in Great Yarmouth. Before the war, two well-used grass tennis courts existed in the grounds of the Old Vicarage near to Rollesby Church, home to a popular tennis club which entered teams in a local village league. These fell into decay during the war and were ploughed up for food production, a fate that befell numerous tennis courts in many of the other Flegg parishes. Few had been replaced by the end of the 1950s. Great Yarmouth was better served with many hard courts for hire along the seafront, although these were in constant use by holidaymakers during the summer. In 1957, under an expansion programme for the school, Yarmouth Grammar School leased a new playing field on the North Denes which included two grass tennis courts and provided tennis coaching to interested sixth-formers as part of the curriculum. My first attempts to become a tennis player took place on these courts and, despite the coaching, it was soon apparent that tennis was not my game. Deftness of touch was not a part of my technique. My game plan was exclusively to hit the ball as hard as possible with little thought for placement. Consequently, I spent more time off the court retrieving lost balls than playing on it. On the few occasions when the ball fell in the opposing player's court, my serve was normally unplayable. Nevertheless, equipped with my grandmother's tennis racket I joined Martham Young Conservatives not for any political purpose but essentially because membership gave access to a privately owned tennis court. There, along with Tim, Bill Brugger and Victor Kemp, I spent many happy summer evenings playing bad tennis and gazing longingly at a bouncy young woman called Claire.

Although opportunities in Rollesby were limited, I was able to take part in many outdoor sports at Yarmouth Grammar School. In the winter, we mainly played football. Rugby was unheard of in our part of East Anglia and, although Yarmouth had a few hockey clubs (roller as well as field hockey) most of my fellow grammar school pupils considered hockey a girls' game, nice to watch but not a game for men. Instead, we played robust and often bloody games of shinty during outside PE sessions – this was considered to be a manly alternative. The inter-house cross country championship took place every year in March over a 3½-mile circular route starting in a field north of the Yarmouth Stadium on Caister Road, meandering over the marshes to Caister Castle and back. Most senior boys took part and spent a month or more beforehand in training. On the command 'Ready, steady, go', bellowed out by the sports master on a megaphone, the race began and all the competitors made a mad dash across the field towards a dyke which, in the wet month of March, was usually filled with water. My first attempt at the cross country ended in disaster when, on arriving at the dyke, I received a push in the back from another competitor and finished up in the obstacle rather than jumping over it. Nevertheless, I did manage to complete the course, wet through, cold and tired, but not last. My best ever performance was in March 1959 when I finished a creditable eighth.

The highlight of the summer term was the school's inter-house athletics championships held at the Wellesley, Yarmouth's premier sports ground, home to the Yarmouth 'Bloaters' football team in the winter, and athletics and cricket in the summer. Competitors waiting for their turn watched the day's events from the grandstand, scrutinised carefully by numerous unemployed form masters and kept up to date with progress via an unintelligible loudspeaker system. Athletics was not my forte, having failed miserably every year to progress beyond the initial heats for most field and track events. But in my final year at senior school I volunteered to compete for South House in the newly introduced hop-step-and-jump. Only one of the competitors displayed any skill at the event and, consequently, to my great surprise I finished in second place, despite my best jump being a full 12ft less than that of the winner, and was awarded with my one and only athletics medal and an unlikely place at the Norfolk School's Athletic Championships. Great Yarmouth had an energetic Athletic Club based at the Wellesley Sports Ground, its popularity enhanced by the national success of two of its athletes, Ted Buswell and Anne Pashley. Like many others, I followed their careers in athletics closely, as both of them had links with Great Yarmouth Grammar School. Ted Buswell was an ex-pupil and Anne Pashley was the daughter of the English Master. In common with the whole of Great Yarmouth, I was ecstatic when Anne Pashley won a silver medal at the 1956 Melbourne Olympics.

In the Flegg villages, competitive indoor sports took place mainly in village halls, school classrooms or the local public house, and were limited by the size and nature of those facilities. I have no recollection of any private or council-owned sports, leisure or health centres in our immediate locality. Squash, golf and country clubs did exist, but expensive membership charges ensured that these were exclusively a facility for the better off. As most local village halls had low ceilings, competitive badminton was not possible and shuttlecock remained a garden-based game for children. Apart from darts, competitive indoor sport was limited mainly to table tennis, billiards and boxing. I played ping-pong against my father on our dining table despite the difficulties of playing in a small room. As a result, any movement was severely restricted during matches – my father usually played standing still with one hand in his pocket – and the game often ended when the ball was hit accidentally onto the open fire. I continued to play table tennis at Yarmouth Grammar School on a table that had been presented to the school by the PTA. I also played table tennis at Rollesby's youth club and at university where I was introduced to innovations such as the penholder grip and sponge bats.

In the early 1950s the most popular cue game was billiards. Teams from the Flegg villages competed in the George Beck Billiards League and played their matches at the local public house or at the village hall. In Great Yarmouth, teams competed in the Yarmouth Billiards League. My father was a keen billiard player and owned a small portable billiard table. We often played keenly contested games in our living room, especially during the Christmas break. By the middle of the 1950s, billiards had become less popular, particularly with younger players, and both the Beck and the Great Yarmouth billiards leagues were disbanded as snooker became the game of choice. Unfortunately, Yarmouth's many snooker halls had become linked with Teddy Boy culture and, as a nervous teenager, I was too cautious to take up the sport. In the 1950s, boxing, the noble art of self-defence, was considered a suitable activity for boys. My father had boxed in the army and was a keen advocate of the sport, following the careers of British boxers like Bruce Woodcock and Freddie Mills closely, as well as supporting the winter

LONDON SCHOOLS' AMATEUR BOXING ASSOCIATION

OFFICIAL PROGRAMME

LONDON v **EAST ANGLIA**
(REGION 1)   (REGION 2)

(QUARTER-FINALS S.A.B.A. NATIONAL CHAMPIONSHIPS)

at

EAST INDIA HALL, POPLAR, E.14

on

SATURDAY, 28th FEBRUARY, 1959

Commencing at 5 p.m.

OFFICIALS:

Officials in Charge..	...	M. C. CRAMER, E. C. AYERS.
Referees and Judges	...	GENTLEMEN OF THE S.A.B.A.
Clerks of Scales ...	...	J. M. JONES, G. TOWNEND.
Medical Officer ...	...	Dr. W. T. DENSHAM RAY.
O.I.C. Seconds ...	...	M. J. McCORMACK
Organising Secretarys	...	R. C. DAVISON, (Region 2)
		E. CHANDLER, (Region 2)
		Hay Currie School, E.14

Martham schoolboy boxers, Carl and Barry Gallant, sparring in a makeshift ring in the school hall. Boxing was encouraged in local schools for exercise and character training. (Stephanie and Barry Gallant)

boxing programmes at the Hippodrome in Great Yarmouth. My only experience of boxing was not a happy one. Armed with two pairs of boxing gloves given to me by Uncle George Miller, I made my way to King George's Playing Field where a competition was organised by a group of older boys using the sandpit as a ring. Unfortunately, during my designated bout, my opponent, deliberately or otherwise, landed a perfect right hook on the end of my chin flooring me for more than the necessary count of ten. Thereafter, my boxing gloves were consigned to a cupboard and I was never tempted to repeat the experience. However, among many of my contemporaries boxing was a popular sport. The Norfolk Schools Amateur Boxing Association, formed in 1950, encouraged boxing in local schools for both exercise and character training. In the 1950s, the possibility of brain damage was not a consideration. Despite primitive conditions and limited resources, Martham School developed a thriving boxing club. Among its many successes were my cousin Stephanie's boyfriend, Barry Gallant, who was a Norfolk County Junior Champion and All England quarter-finalist, and his brother Carl, who, in 1961, progressed to become an All England National Schoolboy Champion at his weight.

ON BEING A SPECTATOR

'A white sports coat', The King Brothers, 1957

As a sport-mad family, we spent many hours listening to sports commentaries on the radio and, eventually, watching sporting programmes on television. International and club football, Test matches, the University Boat Race, the Grand National, Wimbledon and many other events were assiduously followed every year. The radio, TV and cinema newsreels kept us in touch with national sporting highs and lows – Stanley Matthews' Cup Final, the Wembley humiliation at the hands (or feet) of Hungary, Roger Bannister's 4-minute mile, Jim Peters' collapse on the winning line in the Vancouver Commonwealth Games marathon and the Manchester United plane crash at Munich, to mention but a few. My father was particularly addicted to horse racing and listened every evening to the racing results on the radio, marking the day's winners on the racing section in his newspaper. Mother was a football fanatic and insisted on total silence when a match was featured on the radio or TV.

Norwich City supporters at the FA Cup quarter-final at Bramall Lane, Sheffield, February 1959. Among the crowd there are lots of scarves, rattles and rosettes, even a canary in a cage, but no team shirts.
(© Eastern Daily Press 2007)

We also attended live sporting events, mainly those in which we had a particular interest. Mother always watched my father play football and cricket, standing on the sidelines frequently yelling words of encouragement. When my father was not playing, he often took mother and me to watch Yarmouth Town at the Wellesley or Norwich City at Carrow Road. We were among the 9,000 or so spectators who watched Yarmouth Town, from the Eastern Counties League, famously defeat Crystal Palace of the Football League 1–0 in the 1953/4, FA Cup First Round Proper cup-tie. Not that I saw much of the game, as the crowd was so dense that it was almost impossible for a short thirteen-year-old to see any of the action on the pitch. When he finally retired from playing football, my father joined the many spectators supporting a rejuvenated Norwich City Football Club at Carrow Road. Having been saved from bankruptcy by Geoffrey Watling, the club was experiencing some success under the management of Archie Macauley, including a 1959 FA Cup semi-final appearance, an exceptional achievement from a side then in the 3rd Division South of the Football League. At eighteen years of age, I was not always so keen to attend matches with my parents. With them both gainfully occupied at Carrow Road, the coast was clear for me to entertain my girlfriend at home without the fear of any awkward interruptions. However, Wednesday 18 March 1959 is one of the many dates in my life when I know exactly where I was and what I was doing. Like many of my fellow sixth-formers, I stayed away from school so that I could listen with my mother to the radio commentary of the FA Cup semi-final replay between Norwich and Luton Town. Unfortunately Norwich lost 1–0 and mother cried.

Round	Date	Opponent	Score	Played at	Att
1st round	15/11/58	Ilford	3–1	Home	14,084
2nd round	06/12/58	Swindon Town	1–1	Away	14,758
Replay	11/12/58	Swindon Town	1–0	Home	11,724
3rd round	10/01/59	Manchester United	3–0	Home	38,000
4th round	24/01/59	Cardiff City	3–2	Home	38,000
5th round	14/02/59	Tottenham Hotspur	1–1	Away	67,633
Replay	18/02/59	Tottenham Hotspur	1–0	Home	38,000
6th round	28/02/59	Sheffield United	1–1	Away	57,000
Replay	04/03/59	Sheffield United	3–2	Home	38,000
Semi-Final	14/03/59	Luton Town	1–1	White Hart Lane	63,500
Replay	18/03/59	Luton Town	0–1	Birmingham	49,500

Norwich City's FA Cup run, 1958/9 season.

At Leicester, I continued my interest in football on most Saturday afternoons, when I accompanied a group of Southmead residents to the Filbert Street Stadium, home of Leicester City Football Club. As a top division side, the play was regularly of a higher standard than I was used to in Norfolk and I can clearly remember the excitement that I felt on one occasion when I entered the ground to see a game against West Ham featuring their up-and-coming new star, a youthful Bobby Moore. However, most students at Leicester University were more interested in rugby than soccer. The university team was experiencing great success in the inter-varsity rugby league and most of the student body had become caught up with their excitement. Although I was not a rugby fan, I looked forward to the post-match celebrations in the students' bar where I not only learned how to drink vast amounts of alcohol but also the words to many dubious songs such as 'The Wild West Show', 'Eskimo Nell', 'The One-eyed Reilly', 'The Engineer's Song', 'The Sexual Life of a Camel' and the saga of 'Ivan Scavinsky Scavar'. On the few occasions that I was persuaded to visit Welford Road, I watched rugby in total ignorance of its rules surrounded by well-spoken young men in tweed caps, sports jackets, check shirts, cravats and corduroy trousers. By contrast, the football spectators were usually working class men in flat caps, dull overcoats, grey trousers with turn-ups and a muffler tied around their necks. In the 1950s, attendances were high, violence was uncommon and team colours were hardly ever worn by their supporters. The only downside was that standing spectators crowded together on the terraces were an ideal target for pickpockets. My mother had a purse stolen from her handbag during one Norwich City home match.

BOOZE WITH THE BOYS

Come along to the Stork (Welford Road) Friday 7 p.m. and meet the Rugby Club lads. W'imen [sic] not allowed at this stage, but bring any club songs plus your tankard.

'Advert', *Ripple*, Leicester University, 9 October 1959

During the immediate post-war period, speedway became so popular that it almost rivalled football as the country's main spectator sport. A cinder speedway track was constructed at the Yarmouth Stadium, running inside an already long-established grass dog-racing track and, in 1948, the Yarmouth Bloaters speedway team was entered into Division 3 of the National Speedway League. Under the control of promoter Dick Wise, the Bloaters were initially used as a training vehicle for novice riders from Norwich Speedway Club, who were then in Division 2. One young inexperienced rider, Billy Bales, enjoyed so much success with the Bloaters that he became a local hero and his name was inextricably linked with the notion of speed. If my father or I were rushing about, mother often chastised us with the statement 'Who do you think you are – Billy Bales?' For a while the Bloaters enjoyed some success, achieving independence from Norwich and gained promotion to Division 2 in 1949, attracting support from locals and holidaymakers alike. Having been constructed inside the dog circuit, the track was particularly difficult with long straights and very tight corners, giving a definite advantage to the home team. As a result, the Bloaters became infamous for winning most of their home matches while mainly losing away matches.

Aunt Doris Miller was fanatical in her support for the Bloaters and, accompanied by her sisters Muriel and May, attended most midweek home matches during the summer. She regularly brought back a souvenir plastic badge for me; usually in the form of a speedway figure in the colours of the different teams – red and black quarters for Yarmouth and a yellow star on a green background for Norwich – or an imitation motorbike wheel with a rider's picture in the centre. The names of the riders – including Roy Duke, Billy Bales, Sid Hipperson, Reg Morgan, Bill Carruthers, Fred Brand, Barry Briggs and the Rawlinson brothers – became as well known to me as many football players. Unfortunately, the burden of Entertainment Tax and low off-season crowds caused Yarmouth to withdraw from the National League in 1954 and only occasional invitation challenge matches were held at the stadium thereafter, until speedway was finally abandoned in 1961. Personally I was not an avid spectator of speedway. On those occasions when I accompanied Aunt Doris to a match or, in my later teens, joined the gangs of young men seeking female companionship, I found the spectacle boring and noisy, and the smell of oil overpowering. To my shame, my only wish was for an accident to happen in order to relieve the tedium. Accidents did happen with some degree of regularity. Two riders unfortunately died as a result of injuries sustained during Yarmouth's very first competitive season. I much preferred to watch stock car racing. A motor sport seemingly performed with the aim of causing accidents which, despite appearing dramatic, nevertheless resulted in fewer serious injuries to the drivers than occurred in speedway. In the late 1950s, I spent many evenings on the terraces at Yarmouth Stadium with my arm around a girl, listening to loud popular music and watching the antics of the many battered but colourful cars with awe as they careered around the cinder track bashing their way past opponents. Other than football and stock car racing, I much preferred to play sport than watch it.

9

Out in the Open Air

OUT AND ABOUT

'Meet me on the Corner', Max Bygraves, 1956

After work, especially on warm summer evenings and at the weekends, my parents and I spent a lot of time outside just standing around and talking. We often leant against our garden gate, staring up and down the road and chatting to passers-by about nothing in particular. Mother spent hours talking to our next-door neighbour, Mrs Holt, through the back garden hedge or standing at the garden gate nattering to Mrs Evans and Elsie from the farm. My father often walked to the Horse & Groom crossroads to lean against the farm wall, nod at any passing traffic – he apparently knew every driver – and right the world's wrongs in the company of Tom, Sam or Jack. In Great Yarmouth, Grandma Cole rested from her daily chores standing propped up against the frame of her front door, her arms crossed over her ample chest, talking to Mrs Brown from next door, or to Mrs Mulley, from one along. In the 1950s, not only was conversation an important part of our rest and leisure, we also had specific places where we went deliberately to think and talk with others.

As I have already mentioned, the main meeting place for Rollesby's teenagers was the recreation field, especially the veranda of the hut. During the evening and at weekends, even in the cold and dark of winter, a dozen or more teenagers gathered on the veranda to talk, shout, smoke cigarettes and show off in front of the opposite sex. Smaller groups congregated on the benches at the Horse & Groom, outside the refreshment room at the Eels Foot Inn or, for those with a cycle, on the bridge at Potter Heigham where, in the summer, we gazed at the boats on the river and, hopefully, any nubile occupants sunbathing on their decks. Our talk was the talk of teenagers, about music and sport, about life, our fears and our hopes, about boys and about girls, and sometimes about sex. In many ways it was our finishing school with a curriculum of its own, although much of the information, especially about sex (based on hearsay rather than experience) was erroneous and potentially dangerous. Nevertheless, many a boy-girl union was initiated on the veranda of the hut and many a reputation was almost tarnished on the recreation field.

We either cycled or walked around the village. Every day until the age of eleven, I walked the mile to the primary school with my friends, morning and evening, in all weathers, rain, wind or snow, chaperoned only by the older girls and boys.

Most children travelled to and from school unaccompanied by their parents. At Rollesby only the Head Teacher arrived in a car. By the time I reached my teens, I had walked every road, track and footpath in Rollesby and many in the adjoining villages. In the winter, Tony and I often trudged the 2 miles to Martham for an evening film show in the Institute, frequently without the benefit of a torch, or to visit his grandmother at her house on the green. Many villagers went for daily walks, talking with those that they met on the way. Blind Kelly Hodds tapped his way a mile or more every day to fetch his newspaper and shopping from the post office. Richard's uncle marched miles to visit friends, family or a distant hostelry, followed always by Monty his faithful Labrador. After lunch on Sundays, whole families walked together around the village dressed in their best clothes, acquainting themselves with the latest village news and gossip. Young couples walked hand-in-hand along the quieter lanes seeking some privacy to do their courting. I explored the back lanes of many neighbouring villages in the company of a local female, searching for a place to pause and a moment alone. Whether by accident or design, boys and girls were rarely left by themselves in our small and often overcrowded homes. Although I had a bedroom of my own upstairs, containing my radio, record player and personal

BSA

THE BICYCLE YOU CAN'T BEAT!

Three High School girls and the author cycling along Martham Road, Rollesby, 1956. The photograph was taken during a bus strike when we had to ride to Martham station and catch the train to Great Yarmouth before walking to our respective schools. In the 1950s we were expected to attend school no matter what. (Glenda Tooke)

effects, my parents never considered it to be a proper place for entertaining friends, especially girlfriends, so a walk was the only way to be free from their prying eyes.

In the countryside, everybody owned a cycle and going for a cycle ride was a regular leisure time event. With my village friends, I often cycled to the river at Potter Heigham, Ludham or Horning, to the beaches at Hemsby, Horsey, Scratby and Winterton, to the Rollesby, Ormesby and Filby Broads, and, occasionally, even to Great Yarmouth. At various times in my teens I owned numerous cycles, including many made by famous firms such as Raleigh, Hercules, BSA and Triumph, most bought second-hand from the Thursday Acle sale, although I did once build a bike of my own, a drop-handled racing bike made from parts salvaged mostly from a local rubbish dump. In the days when most teenagers could not afford a car, walking or cycling were the main means of travel to village events – cricket and football matches, film shows, whist drives and dances. Cycles were left propped up against a wall, a tree, or a hedge, often two or three deep, or just laid flat on the ground. My parents and I stored our cycles in an unlocked garden shed without any thought that they might be stolen. Cycle clubs existed locally and we were often treated to the sight of hoards of colourfully adorned riders sweeping through the village. Mother once gave bed and breakfast to a lone young cyclist from London who was on a sightseeing tour of East Anglia. When money was tight, Uncle Stanley Cole cycled from Birmingham to Great Yarmouth for his annual visit to see Grandma Cole – a feat not achieved without some considerable discomfort.

SPRING IS HERE, THE COUNTRYSIDE AWAITS YOU. GET OUT AND ABOUT ON A BICYCLE

Cycling is the perfect way to enjoy the sights of the country. For the bicycle is quite silent, it is light and easily manhandled, it is quick and it entails a moderate outlay. On top of all that there is the wind on your face and the pleasant exercise which keep you healthy and happy, and when it is all over and you return home, you have a very satisfying feeling of achievement.

Yarmouth Mercury, 24 April 1959

LEISURE TIME ON THE BROADS

'Gone Fishing', Bing Crosby & Louis Armstrong, 1951

Although most localities have their charms, I deem myself lucky to have spent my youth living in Rollesby, a picturesque village in the district known as the Fleggs. The Fleggs were once an island surrounded by sea and marsh, which was colonised in the late ninth century by King Guthrum's invading Danish army. This fact is supported by the numerous villages and hamlets with the 'by' ending that is indicative of a Danish settlement – Rollesby, Hemsby, Scratby, Ormesby, Filby, Clippesby, Thrigby and Oby. Today, the Fleggs are bounded by the coast to the east; and the river Bure, its tributary the Ant, flat marshland and numerous small lakes, the result of medieval peat digging, to the north, south and west. These lakes are now collectively known as the Northern Norfolk Broads. Consequently, with Trinity

Broad on my doorstep, the river and sea a short distance away, it was natural that activities involving water should form a large element in my teenage leisure pursuits.

Swimming was not one of my most favourite sports. Most of my father's family were good swimmers who plunged into the Broad from off the jetty at the Field or the side of grandfather's rowing boat. Like many of my Yarmouth cousins, I had a definite aversion to water and swallowed mouthfuls every time my head ducked under the surface. Mother was keen that I should learn to swim and enrolled me into classes at the Great Yarmouth swimming pool, an open-air salt-water pool on the seafront. Despite many hours at the pool, I was never able to conquer my fear of the water. After each lesson, my cousin Deanna and I attempted to convince our mothers that we were able to swim by simulating breaststroke in the shallow end of the pool with one foot placed firmly on the bottom. No doubt we were a great disappointment to Deanna's mother, Aunt Doris Parnell, who was an excellent swimmer and had, in her younger days, taken part in the annual sea swim between Yarmouth's Britannia and Wellington piers. With persistence, I was eventually able to make passable attempts at swimming back and breaststrokes, always with my head held high above the surface. However, no matter whether in the pool or the Broad, I preferred to swim alone, lacking both the ability and the confidence to join in the water frolics of my friends. I gained some consolation from knowing that the coxswain of the Cromer lifeboat was also a poor swimmer. However, many of my friends were excellent swimmers. One Grammar School boy, David Liffen, gained notoriety by becoming the youngest person to conquer the treacherous currents off Yarmouth's seashore and swim the 2 miles or so out to the Scroby Sands, a sandbank in the North Sea, and back.

I much preferred to be in a boat on the Broads. When I was on my own I often rowed grandfather's boat out onto Rollesby Broad which, in the 1950s, was a quiet contemplative place to be and a haven for wildlife. As it was separate from the main Broadland waterways it was free from the yacht and motor cruiser traffic associated with the holiday industry, and the only vessels to be seen were a few rowing boats containing local fishermen, naturalists and, occasionally, the more energetic holidaymaker. In the days before widespread environmental pollution, even the smallest sailing boats were denied untroubled access to the waters of Trinity Broad by many islands of water lilies. With little to disturb them, birds of all kinds found sanctuary on the water – great crested grebes, ducks, moorhens, coots, herons, swans, over-wintering geese and even an occasional bittern. Otters inhabited the banks. Towards the end of the decade, this natural order was disturbed by the arrival of the coypu, large brown rat-like invaders from the Americas, escapees from fur farms. My father once managed to trap a coypu at the Field and, for months afterwards, its large body lay decaying on the ground, a sight he proudly exhibited to anyone who expressed an interest.

Although sail boats were a common sight on the rest of the rivers and Broads, and, like many local residents, I watched the annual regattas at Potter Heigham, Thurne and Horning with interest, I had neither the opportunity nor the necessary finances to become a yachtsman. Indeed, my one and only venture into sailing ended in ignominy and embarrassment. One weekend, Richard and I were permitted

Rowing boats could be hired by the hour or the day from boathouses at the Eels Foot Inn and the Sportsman's Arms. (Author's Collection)

to borrow a small dingy belonging to some friends of Richard's parents. Undoubtedly they were unaware that neither of us had ever sailed a dingy before, and we were certainly not going to tell them. Once on board, we pushed off from the riverbank and, with some trepidation, pulled on the appropriate ropes to raise the small white sail up the mast. With beginners' luck and a slight breeze behind us, we sailed perfectly down the river from Thurne towards Potter Heigham, waving nonchalantly at the fishermen and walkers along the riverbank. Unfortunately, pride came before a fall. After a reasonable distance, the river took a sharp turn to the right. On approaching the bend we failed to understand that making a turn in a boat was not accomplished by merely turning the rudder. As we entered the corner, the breeze came in sideways, filled the sail and tipped the boat over and us into the water. Eventually, with a great deal of panic-assisted effort, we managed to right the boat before it sank and hurriedly pulled down the sail. Our return back to Thurne was by oar power rather than sail and our bedraggled state elicited much laughter from the fishermen on the bank.

The most popular water-based sport locally was fishing. Most men and boys owned a fishing rod, the boys fishing from the shoreline, the bridge or the jetty at the Eels Foot Inn, while the men fished mainly from rowing boats. My first fishing rod was put together by my father and consisted of a simple wooden pole with a line tied to the end with a float, weights and a hook attached. I spent many hours fishing with this rod off the end of the jetty at the Field with little success. Eventually, Grandfather Miller gave me a four-piece fishing rod with a cork handle. An automatic reel was attached to the rod with shiny metal rings. Despite not being fanatical about fishing, I regularly joined my Uncles Cecil and George on fishing expeditions in grandfather's boat. Uncle George Miller was a keen fisherman and spent at least two one-week long holidays in Rollesby, fishing every day. I enjoyed their company and the opportunity to share the contents of their hip flasks, a necessary perk on cold mornings. Both uncles competed against each other for the

largest number of fish caught during the day, each keeping their catch in keepnets hung from the stern of the boat. At the end of the session, the nets were weighed, the results noted and the fish returned to the water. Damaged fish were usually taken home as a treat for our domestic cats. Occasionally, fishing competitions were organised on the Broad or along the riverbank at Potter Heigham. Often a hundred or more keen fishermen spent all day, often hidden under large umbrellas in the rain, peering intently at a bobbing float in the water. A few fishermen had bells on the end of their rods to warn when a fish had been hooked, presumably a precaution in case they went to sleep. In 1949, the All England Freshwater Championship was held on the River Thurne, near Potter Heigham, when over 1,000 fishermen took

Family members fishing and swimming from grandfather's boat. We used Rollesby Broad as a recreational facility as often as we could. The rafts of lily pads made fishing and swimming difficult in places. (Author's Collection)

part. A few of my friends preferred sea fishing, either from the beaches at Hemsby and Winterton, or off the ends of Great Yarmouth's two piers. I was never tempted to join them as sea fishing sessions always seemed to start well before dawn. Nevertheless, I often watched them in action, fascinated by the methods they used to cast the line immense distances out to sea, usually by flinging the weighted line backwards over their heads.

ANGLING MATCH

The newly formed Rollesby Angler's Club held its end of season prize competition on Sunday when 28 anglers competed for eight prizes. In a fleet of 14 boats members set out in a thick fog for the numbered positions they had drawn on stakes set by the starter and organiser, Mr G. Skoyles. Mr G. Dawson with a bream of 2lb 9oz won the prize for the largest fish and also with his companion the boat prize for the heaviest bag. Mr Dawson also had the largest roach. The prize for the greatest number of fish per boat was won by Mr F. Nichols' boat with 35 roach, including also the prize for the smallest fish. The prize for the largest silver bream was won by Mr E. Skoyles and the smallest silver bream by Mr Alexander. The prize for the largest perch was won by Mr E. Church with the only perch caught. Mr C. Miller was in charge of the scales and Mr G. Skoyles who is water bailiff for the Broads was thanked for his assistance as organiser.

Village News, Rollesby, *Yarmouth Mercury*, 16 October 1953

Uncle Cecil Miller, a member of the Rollesby Anglers' Club, fishing on the Little Ormesby Broad. Fishing was a popular pastime among the village men and boys. Most weekends, many youths and boys fished from off Rollesby Bridge, the jetties at the Sportsman's Arms and Eels Foot, and along the banks of the broad. (Stephanie and Barry Gallant)

THE VILLAGE YEAR

'Magic Moments', Perry Como, 1958

Routinely, various annual celebrations and festivals were held in the village, usually associated with religious, historic or local events. In 1950s Rollesby, most residents, if asked, would claim to be Christian – mainly Church of England, Methodist or Catholic – and supportive of church-organised activities. Although in my early years I attended Sunday school most weeks and sung in the church choir, I could not admit to being a devout Christian. Like my parents, I went to church for baptisms, weddings and funerals, and for special occasions throughout the year. My attendance at church owed more to the social nature of the activity than to any demonstration of religious belief. For some, going to church was not only their Christian duty but also a welcome opportunity to meet and converse with other people. In our family, Grandfather Miller was a committed member of the Church of England and delighted in his role as the People's Churchwarden. But, he also enjoyed attending weekly church services for the singing – he loved singing hymns at the top of his voice, all too frequently out of tune – and the pre- and post-service chat in the churchyard. In my teens I went to church infrequently, usually only at Easter and Christmas and for the popular and well-attended services on Mothering Sunday, Harvest Thanksgiving and Remembrance Day.

In order to foster more public interest in the Church, our vicar, who was newly installed in the parishes of Rollesby, Fleggburgh and Clippesby, attempted to reintroduce the community-based services traditionally held on Plough and Rogation Sundays. Plough Sunday, the first Sunday after twelfth night, was considered to be the start of the agricultural year and the time to break the soil with a plough. During the service, a plough was brought into the church and blessed. On Rogation Sunday, the fourth Sunday in Lent, a service was conducted in the open air, when various fields and allotments were visited by the congregation in procession and prayers were offered for a good harvest. Historically, Rogation Sunday was the day for walking around the village boundary and cleaning boundary marker stones. I liked Mothering Sunday because it was a day when the family met together, usually for tea at Hall Cottages with my grandparents. At the morning service, mothers were given posies of wild snowdrops, violets or primroses picked from hedgerows and gardens by their children. Other than the Christmas carol service, I enjoyed Harvest Thanksgiving the most. The church was always decorated with flowers and sheaves of corn, and in front of the altar and down the aisle, a display of fruit, vegetables, bread, eggs and jars of jam and pickles. Everybody in the congregation brought an offering which they added to the displays. I usually brought a basket full of apples picked from the trees in our garden. The service included many of my favourite hymns and I joined grandfather in singing at the top of my voice thanksgiving classics such as 'We plough the fields and scatter', 'Praise my soul the King of Heaven' and 'All things bright and beautiful'.

HARVEST THANKSGIVING

Services were held at St George's Church Rollesby on Friday evening when the preacher was the Rev H.C. Kemp, Vicar of Martham. The services were continued on Sunday and were conducted by the Rector (Rev H. Gascoigne). Mrs E. Notley sang solos at each of the services. On Sunday afternoon, a children's gift service was held. Their gifts together with the fruit, flowers, vegetables, eggs and preserves with which the church was decorated were sent to the Fisherman's Hospital at Yarmouth.

'Village news, Rollesby', *Yarmouth Mercury*, 30 September 1955

Although many social changes were taking place during the 1950s, Rollesby was still primarily a traditional agricultural community and harvest time was an event of major importance. Older children were often allowed time off from school to help in the fields. Every year in my early teens, Richard and I helped to stack sheaves of corn into stooks and load trailers to transport the corn to the stack yard on his father's farm. At other times I drove the tractor, even though I was only sixteen years old. The end of harvest was always celebrated, not only by the Harvest Thanksgiving service but also by various treats given by the farmers to those that helped at harvest time, such as harvest home money bonuses, outings, gifts and suppers. There was also an annual Harvest Ball at the Floral Hall in Gorleston.

HARVEST HOME SUPPER

On Saturday Mr & Mrs W.R. Chapman entertained the employees of their Martham & Rollesby farms to a harvest home supper in the barn at Clarke's Farm. Mr Chapman, in welcoming his guests, paid a tribute to the men's work in gathering in the harvest and spoke of the excellent feeling between the staff and himself. He thanked the men for helping to win the Stalham Farmer's Sugar Beet Challenge Cup which was on view on the centre table. Mr Chapman mentioned that Mr J. Moore was retiring from the position of farm foreman, although he was not giving up work, and Mrs Chapman presented him with a clock. From the staff Mr Moore received a barometer. Entertainment was provided by Mr Jack Rogers and Miss Phyllis Holden, formerly of 'Showtime'.

'Village news, Martham', *Yarmouth Mercury*, 5 October 1951

Other events and festivals helped to break up the routine of our village year. As a boy I looked forward to 14 February, Valentine's Day, not for any romantic reason but for the local tradition of leaving anonymous gifts on the doorstep, normally for the children of the house. After tea on Valentine's Day, I usually sat waiting and hoping for a knock on the door. When one came it was normally accompanied by my name being called through the letterbox or keyhole. Whoever knocked was always long gone by the time the door was opened but had usually left a small personal gift on the doorstep. Occasionally the gift was a trick, a large well-wrapped package containing a sweet or a nut. When asked who had left it, mother always said Jimmy Valentine. Others at various times suggested that the mysterious benefactor was Jack Valentine or Jack Frost. Sometimes, even the adults were rewarded. I can remember once when Grandfather Miller was suffering from a cold, his anonymous benefactor left him a tin of Zubes. In my late teens, Valentine's Day was celebrated in the normal way by sending and receiving unsigned romantic cards. As they were usually anonymous, it was never possible to be totally sure who had sent any that arrived through the post. If only one arrived, then it was safe to assume that it was from a current girlfriend. Two or more cards often resulted in embarrassment and confusion. It was always best just to feel admired but to say nothing. However, as Tim and I frequently sent unsigned cards with saucy inscriptions to males we disliked, we were never sure if those received were also a joke.

On Shrove Tuesday, mother always made thin pancakes in her frying pan. My father and I often managed to eat six or more each, all soaked with a liberal dose of lemon juice – sometimes squeezed from a yellow lemon-shaped bottle – and covered in sugar. On 1 April my friends and I played jokes on one another, often silly immature teenage jokes that only we found funny. At Easter we ate chocolate eggs, hollow eggs bought from Woolworth's that were patterned and covered in colourful silver foil. At primary school, all the children painted designs on boiled eggs to take home as an Easter present for their mothers. On Easter Sunday we always had tea at Hall Cottages with my Miller grandparents. Every year, as part of the high tea spread, we were served a pink blancmange moulded to the form of an Easter rabbit. On 5 November, all the family went to the village bonfire held on a field adjacent to King George's Playing Field. When everyone had let off their fireworks, potatoes and chestnuts were cooked in the fire. The teenage boys took great delight in setting off bangers, usually in an attempt to frighten the teenage girls. Many a reassuring arm around an intimidated girl was the starting point for a teenage romance. On Remembrance Sunday, we paraded in front of Rollesby's war memorial at St George's Church. In the 1950s, memories of the two world wars were still strong and the memorial service was well attended, many, like my grandmother, remembering their fallen relatives. Grandfather Miller was an active member of the Fleggburgh & District British Legion, a branch numbering nearly 150 members, and often carried the Legion's flag at the service. Throughout the 1950s, my mother helped Grandmother Miller to organise the village poppy appeal collection. Despite having served in the army during the Italian campaign, my father never attended the service but always observed the two minutes silence at eleven o'clock, no matter where he was at the time.

REMEMBRANCE SERVICES IN THE VILLAGES. ROLLESBY REMEMBERS

At Rollesby a service was held around the war memorial where the silence was observed and the names of the dead were read. The address was given by Rev H. Gascoigne, chaplain of the Fleggburgh branch of the British Legion which includes Rollesby and district. Members of the branch attended the service and Capt D.G. Tacon led the parade. Mr H. Curtis carried the standard. The collection of £2 2s 2d was added to the parish collection to make a total of £10 17s. Mrs G. Miller organised the collection and collectors were Miss S. Miller, Miss V. Tubby and Mr C.R. Miller.

'Village news, Rollesby', *Yarmouth Mercury*, 15 November 1956

In the summer, every Flegg village organised a summer fête to raise money for the upkeep of one of its communal facilities – the church, village hall or playing field. Often the fête was combined with a keenly contested annual flower, fruit and vegetable show in which village residents competed in various gardening categories for trophies and small money prizes. Fêtes were normally held on a Saturday afternoon at village recreation fields and opened by a local celebrity or an invited artist who was appearing in one of Great Yarmouth's summer variety shows. Most village clubs and societies contributed in some way to the fête, either by organising a sideshow, a stall or assisting with the refreshments. Everybody was involved either as an organiser, helper or participant on the day. My mother, grandparents and I usually attended most of the local fêtes including those at Rollesby, Martham, Fleggburgh and Ormesby. My father was normally too busy. Rollesby's village fête was held every year in June or July at King George's Playing Field and included stalls, sideshows and special events. Different individuals and village groups manned the various stalls which normally included a white elephant stall selling bric-a-brac, a cake stall selling buns, tarts, sponges and cakes, a gardener's stall with plants, vegetables and flowers and an ice-cream cart. Competitions involved trying to throw ping-pong balls into an enamelled bucket, attempting to get the highest score when throwing three well-used darts at a dartboard, knocking the most skittles down with three balls, trying to roll balls through hoops, rolling pennies at targets to win money prizes, trying to beat the goalkeeper with a penalty kick, guessing the name

Richard's entry into the best-decorated bicycle competition, Rollesby Fête, 1950. The multi-functional 'hut' that was erected on the recreation field immediately after the war is clearly visible behind. (Richard Tacon)

of a doll, the number of peas in a bottle and the weight of a piglet. There was always a treasure hunt in the sandpit and a prize draw. The horticultural aspect of Rollesby's fêtes ceased soon after the war when the gardening club folded, and was replaced by exhibitions of arts, crafts and hobbies. Teas and cakes were prepared and sold in the hut by members of the Ladies' Club. Every year special attractions were organised, which at different times included 'bonny baby' and knobbliest knees competitions, slow cycle races, cycle speedway, children's races, fancy dress and best-decorated bicycle events, Punch & Judy shows and comic cricket matches. The evening usually ended with a social and dance in the school.

CHURCH FETE

The annual fête in aid of Fleggburgh and Billockby Church funds was held on the Recreation Ground on Saturday. It was opened by Miss Beryl Reid of 'Showtime' who was introduced by Dr T.W.E. Royden and thanked by the Rector (Rev R.A. Atkins) and Mr J. Clarke. Chief among the main attractions was a flower, fruit and vegetable show which drew a record number of entries. This was judged by Messers Allard of Rollesby. There was also an ankle competition judged by Mr Alan Shires of 'Showtime'. The winner was Miss A. Newman. There were 18 entries for the fancy dress parade which was judged by Miss Reid. As usual the fête was followed by a social in the village hall.

'Village news, Fleggburgh', *Yarmouth Mercury*, 18 August 1950

FETE & GYMKHANA

A fête and gymkhana held on the Coronation Recreation ground on Wednesday of last week raised £184 for the Playing Field fund. The event, which drew a crowd of over a 1,000, was opened by Mrs Jack Jay of the Windmill Theatre, who introduced Tommy Trinder. Mrs Francis (fête Hon. Secretary) had provided numerous sideshows, entertainments and competitions, and the gymkhana arranged by Mr W.R. Chapman proved a great attraction. 'Uncle Rex' compeered a concert party. Mr & Mrs Roy Francis found ready customers at the goldfish stall. Mrs G. Temple and helpers had a busy time serving refreshments. Mrs Bradfield supervised a fancy dress parade and Mr M.A. Wakeman had an array of stalls and sideshows which were looked after by members of his staff and pupils. Tony Dowe, the young Martham Cricket Club batsman, defended his wickets at the nets so successfully against all comers that they were only hit twice. During the evening a social and dance arranged by Mr Roy Francis was held in the Institute where music was provided by the Ace of Clubs band. The proceeds included receipts from a bowls tournament held on Mr Ansell's green and a whist drive was organised by Mrs Myhill.

'Village news, Martham', *Yarmouth Mercury*, 9 September 1955

EVENTS IN TOWN

'Strawberry Fair', Anthony Newley, 1960

Being a holiday town, there was always plenty to see and do in Great Yarmouth. However, two annual events that were a great draw for villagers, including myself, were the Easter Fair and September's Battle of Britain Week. The Easter Fair was held annually on the market place during the first Friday and Saturday after Easter. Every year without fail I journeyed by bus with my teenage friends to enjoy the attractions of the fairground – the sounds, the sights, the excitement and the gangs of girls that giggled their way from one scary ride to the next. The fair occupied most of the market place and the plains in front of Lacon's Brewery and the bomb-damaged St Nicholas' Church. The permanent stalls remained only at the top end of the market place, notably the fish and chip, confectionary and seafood stalls that did a roaring trade with the visiting fairgoers. The main attractions were lined up along the centre of the market place – colourfully decorated roundabouts with exotic names such as the Skid, the Whip, the Whirl, and the Ben Hur Speedway that gave breathtaking switchback rides to hoards of screaming teenagers, accompanied by loud fairground organ music. Alongside these were waltzers, the cakewalk, chair-o-planes, dodgems and gallopers, and, in the centre, the Mat, a tower that dominated the middle of the fairground around which a smooth metal slide spiralled from top to bottom and down which children and adults descended sat on a small mat. On either side there were sideshows where contestants tried their luck at hitting targets with darts or rifles, threw balls at coconuts or attempted to ring prizes with hoops, usually without success. Smaller rides for children, powered by an attendant turning a wheel, were scattered through the fairground. At the church end of the fair there were ranks of swinging boats and large highly decorated caravans: the living quarters of the fairground families. In some of the caravans, elderly women dressed in gypsy outfits read palms and predicted fortunes for sixpence a go. Novelty booths covered the Brewery Plain: boxing booths where any challenger could try to box for three rounds with a resident fighter and tents making exhibitions out of human deformities – fat people, bearded women and tiny dwarfs. Behind the stalls huge generators hummed continuously as they produced the power to drive the rides and illuminate the hundreds of coloured light bulbs that covered every roundabout and stall, linked by miles of thick black cables that snaked across the fairground often tripping up unobservant visitors. At the end of the weekend, the fair dispersed into smaller units which toured around the country villages and market towns throughout the summer months. Periodically small fairs arrived at Martham Green and Fleggburgh's Recreation Field to do good trade with the local youth.

KEYNOTE OF EASTER FAIR WAS SPEED

The Easter Fair, which has attracted crowds from Yarmouth and the outlying districts for four centuries, has come and gone. It arrived in a stream of immaculate caravans and painted trailers and by Thursday most of the giant high speed roundabouts, cake walks, swing-boats, stalls, shies and palmists' mysterious tents had been erected on the Market Place. While the showmen worked they were surrounded by crowds of admiring children, many of whom were allowed to sample the delights of 'Ben Hur's Speedway', 'The Marathon' and the 'Dodgems' before the Fair opened officially on Friday. On Friday afternoon, buses having been diverted, the Market Place was manned with excited children, exhausted parents and employees from nearby shops who had slipped out for a quick look. Nearly every child had a paper hat, a tinsel trimmed umbrella or was sucking on a cloud of pink 'candy floss' wound round a stick. A steady stream of small boys whirled down 'The Mat' which towered above the awnings of the 'Try your luck; four shots a tanner' stalls. Barney and Joy, a mountainous couple weighing 68 stones between them, proved a big attraction.

Yarmouth Mercury, 29 April 1949

The grand finale to the summer holiday season was Great Yarmouth's annual Battle of Britain Week, a ten-day-long festival in early September held as part of the national celebrations to commemorate the famous battle of the Second World War, and organised by the RAF Association for the benefit of the RAF Benevolent Fund. The many events held during the festival were always well supported, not only by large audiences from the local population and visiting holidaymakers but also through the active participation of the many stars appearing in Yarmouth's summer shows, making Yarmouth's contribution one of the largest and most profitable of all the celebrations held throughout the country. Despite taking place during school term time, children of all ages took part in the festivities. While still at school, I attended many of the events held over the two weekends of the festival. In the Septembers of 1959 and 1960, the festival helped to bridge the quiet gap between summer holiday work and the start of Leicester University's autumn term.

Of the twenty or more activities that took place during the festival – activities that included roller hockey matches, roller-skating displays, boat races on the River Yare, a celebrity football match at the Wellesley ground, darts tournaments, dancing displays, an Old Tyme Fancy Dress Ball at the Wellington Pier Winter Gardens, a Monster Swimming Gala, a Carnival Ball at the Floral Hall and a concluding Thanksgiving Service – my favourite events were the balloon races, the competition for the title of Miss Battle of Britain, the Carnival procession and the Festival of East

Miss Norfolk Candy at the Goodes Hotel, 1958. Cousin Margaret (third from the right) took part and came third. (John and Margaret White)

Miss Great Yarmouth, 1950. A dazzled Frankie Howerd announces the result of the Miss Great Yarmouth beauty contest at the Marina. (© Eastern Daily Press 2007)

Coast Jazz, the last of which became a feature of the festival from 1959. On many occasions I bought a helium-filled balloon from the kiosk in front of the Marina concert hall, completed the attached tag and released it to join the line of other balloons climbing high into the sky and out to sea. The winner of the major prize was the owner of the balloon that travelled the furthest distance from Yarmouth, assuming that its finder understood the written instructions and returned the tag to the organisers as requested. Naturally, I never won but the balloons of those that did frequently travelled great distances – some were returned from Italy and Yugoslavia. Mother enjoyed the Miss Battle of Britain bathing beauty contest that was normally held inside the Marina during the week and watched by over 1,000 spectators. I often sat with her on the Marina's canvas chairs, admiring the bevy of swimsuited young women posing in front of the judges. The winner was usually presented with her crown by a visiting celebrity and paraded in an open carriage along the promenade. In the 1950s, political correctness was not an issue and bathing beauty competitions were common. In addition to Miss Battle of Britain, Yarmouth hosted

Miss Great Yarmouth and Miss Gorleston as well as Miss Poppet, Miss Norfolk Candy and Miss Smith's Crisps. Every year without fail, mother watched Eric Morley's Miss World on television. My father and I watched too, but undoubtedly from a different perspective.

The highlight of the week was the Carnival procession which was normally held on the Thursday afternoon, a long cavalcade of decorated floats, cars and cycles accompanied by military bands, children and adults in fancy dress encouraging the watching public to add their contributions to their collecting tins. Assembling each year at the Beaconsfield Recreation Ground, the procession normally made its way along the sea front to the Pleasure Beach, back again to Regent Road, over the Haven Bridge and along Southtown Road, ending a three-hour journey at the Floral Hall in Gorleston. The most spectacular of all Yarmouth's Carnival processions was the one that I witnessed in September 1960. Led by a float carrying the Carnival King and Queen, a second float promoting Miss Battle of Britain and her handmaidens followed by the civic car containing the mayor and mayoress, the 1960 procession involved over eighty motorised floats and five bands, including the energetic rhythmic marching band of the American 3rd Air Force, and

Great Yarmouth's 1960 Battle of Britain Carnival procession passing in front of the Queens Hotel on Regent Street. (© Eastern Daily Press 2007)

St Faith's programme, Battle of Britain Week, 1953.

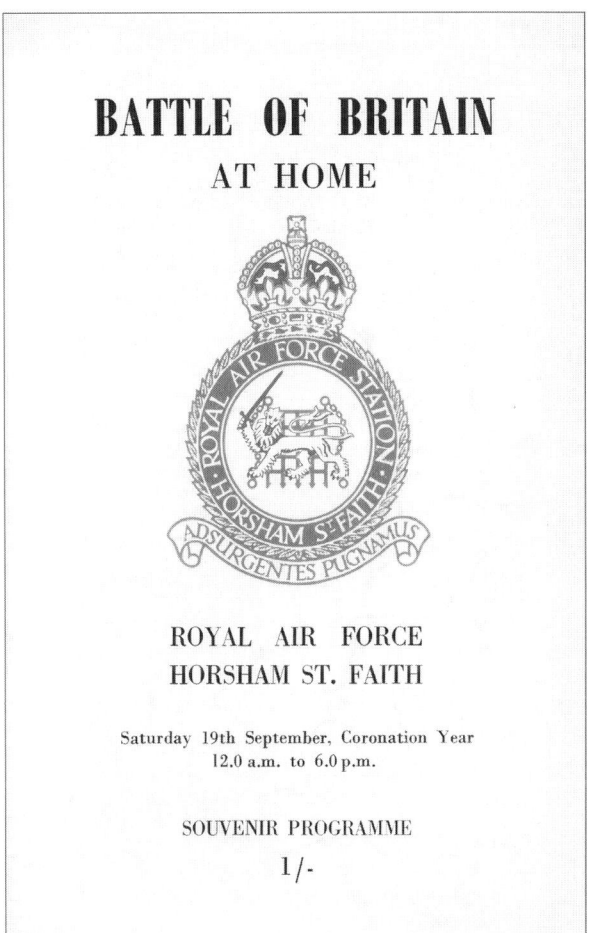

BATTLE OF BRITAIN
AT HOME

ROYAL AIR FORCE
HORSHAM ST. FAITH

Saturday 19th September, Coronation Year
12.0 a.m. to 6.0 p.m.

SOUVENIR PROGRAMME
1/-

was considered at the time to be the largest ever held anywhere in the country. Some of the floats represented Yarmouth's various summer shows and carried many of their performing stars on their tableau. As part of the festivities, many of Norfolk's military airfields had open days with flying displays and static exhibits. At the age of sixteen, I was fanatical about military aircraft, so during the Battle of Britain Week celebrations in 1956 my parents took me to an open day at Horsham St Faith's aerodrome as a treat for passing my O level examinations and gaining entry into the sixth form at Great Yarmouth Grammar School.

HORSHAM ST FAITH

St Faiths has been given priority in the allocation of aircraft and equipment for a display and an impressive line-up is planned. Included in the fly-past are four of the new 'V' bombers – the Victor and Valliant – recently come into service with Bomber Command, Javelin and Venom fighters, and one of the famous Comets; now being used by Transport Command. Highlight of the flying displays will be request aerobatics by a Provost training aircraft for which the instructions from the public will be relayed into the aircraft by radio telephone. Displays will also be given by Hawker Hunter as well as the No 74 Squadron Meteor aerobatic team, the only squadron based at St Faith that took part in the fly-past when Princess Margaret visited the aerodrome six weeks ago. Ground displays will include 14 British and American aircraft and there will be demonstrations of the Martin-Baker ejector seat.

Eastern Daily Press, 7 September 1956

10

Visits, Outings & Holidays

VISITS & TRIPS

'If I knew you were coming I'd've baked a cake', Eve Young, 1950

With so many friends and family living in Rollesby and Great Yarmouth, visiting them in their homes was a regular occurrence. Many visits were unplanned and made on the spur of the moment with no prior warning, mainly because most of my relatives and friends had no telephone. Nevertheless, whether alone or in company, I was normally greeted warmly and I was treated to tea, biscuits and conversation, no matter what task had been interrupted by my arrival. Whenever mother or I travelled into Yarmouth, our first stop was always at Grandma Cole's house on North Market Road. Mother visited her every Wednesday and Saturday without fail. As many of the Cole family also visited her on a Saturday morning, it was an ideal opportunity to meet up and talk with my aunts, uncles and cousins; Aunt Doris Parnell with my cousin Deanna, Aunt Edie Hammond – always protesting that she 'can't stop, can't stop, I'm in a hurry' but never leaving without having had a cup of tea – and, occasionally, Uncles Edward and Bob. When Uncles Arthur and Stanley made their annual visits from Birmingham with their families to stay at North Market Road, everybody came to see them, frequently arriving at the same time to join a noisy and excited gathering crowded into grandma's small front room. In Rollesby, hardly a day went by when I did not pay a visit to my Miller grandparents at Hall Cottages or to Aunt Doris Miller at the post office, often walking through their unlocked doors without knocking as if walking into my own home.

When a visit was pre-planned, the hospitality was even more generous. For a morning visit, my parents and I were offered milky coffee or tea with biscuits and, in the afternoon, tea with sandwiches (usually ham when it was available) and, sometimes, cake which we consumed while sat in comfortable armchairs with our plates balanced on our knees. If we were invited for a meal it was always at the weekend and for tea – hardly ever for dinner, which was traditionally eaten at midday on Saturdays and Sundays by most of my relatives. My parents and I often had Sunday tea with my Miller grandparents, usually after a ride out in my father's car.

Every year, Uncle Stanley Cole and his family combined a visit home from Birmingham with a seaside holiday. Note the seaside fashions worn in 1953. (Author's Collection)

To start the meal we were served with sandwiches, usually ham or salmon and occasionally both, or, if these were not available, a suitable alternative such as cheese, tomato, cucumber, potted meat or shrimp paste. I cannot say that I was a keen sandwich eater and preferred other fillings to the monotonous ham, salmon or paste. Occasionally, grandmother would give in to my whims and provide jam, chocolate spread or condensed milk sandwiches – I even enjoyed her experiment with Bovril and lettuce as a combined filling. My grandmother's sandwiches were legendary. Despite always wearing gloves to prepare the tea (her hands were badly affected with eczema), she managed to cut wafer thin slices of bread which were then covered sparingly with butter, a feat that she achieved by first warming the butter on a saucer under the grill. Once filled, each of her sandwiches (which were cut neatly into triangular quarters) was barely a decent mouthful. Sandwiches were followed by jelly and blancmange; each made in a mould and tipped onto a serving dish to resemble two wobbly castles. At grandmother's teas, jelly and blancmange were eaten with bread, often brown bread, a convention not to my taste. Finally, as my grandmother had a very sweet tooth, we were given cakes, mainly shop-bought cakes that were a long-anticipated treat – cream horns, chocolate éclairs, meringues, very sickly pastries called Kunzles, coffee Japs and iced cupcakes, and, in the centre of the table placed on a glass stand, a sponge, a Battenberg or a Dundee fruit cake. After tea, everybody talked and played cards and games before going home. When any members of either family made visits to Rollesby or Great Yarmouth, tea parties were always held in their honour with a dozen or more of their relatives attending. At Hall Cottages, summer tea parties were often held outside on the lawn with the food laid out on trestle tables, despite the ever-present hazard of wasps and flies. For entertainment we played clock golf, shuttlecock or took part in a treasure hunt around the garden that was normally devised by my grandmother. Mother enjoyed parties and used every excuse to invite our relatives to tea. Although these parties were lively and enjoyable, my parents drank little and, other than at Christmas, rarely provided much in the way of alcoholic drink for their visitors. Beer and spirits allegedly gave my father migraines and my mother had the reputation of becoming tipsy after just one Snowball. At one of mother's summer parties, Uncle Stanley Cole, being in need of a long cool drink, volunteered to take our dog, Rover, for a walk. Ten minutes after their departure, Rover returned collarless. Fearing that Uncle Stanley may have met with an accident I was sent to look for him. Fifty yards away I discovered Rover's lost lead and collar tied to one of the pillars of the Horse & Groom's entrance porch. Inside the Horse & Groom, Uncle Stanley was finishing a thirst-quenching pint of Lacon's Best Bitter unaware that Rover had escaped. Thirty minutes later, we both returned to the party refreshed.

For those who owned a motorcar, 'going for a ride' was a regular event. My parents went for a Sunday drive in my father's car after lunch, winter and summer alike. Their destination was either the seaside, a local beauty spot, a location that was in the news or my father's latest building project. Not that they went far as, in common with most Flegg drivers of a certain age, my father drove his car no faster than 40 miles an hour, usually in the middle of the road. Our favourite seaside destinations were Winterton, Hemsby and California Cliffs, where we walked on the beach, collected seashells and threw stones at the sea. After stormy weather, we sometimes travelled to the more northerly villages of Happisburgh, Walcott and Mundesley to look for signs of coastal erosion, which often involved spectacular cliff collapses. At Yarmouth, we parked at the harbour's mouth to look at the sea crashing against the breakwater and to watch passing ships on the skyline. In October each year, we drove slowly along the quay, marvelling at the site of the visiting herring fishing fleet which was moored from the harbour's mouth to the Town Hall, often three or four boats deep. In 1953 we joined many other sightseers taking in the tragic effects of the infamous East Coast floods. Occasionally we travelled further afield, normally on day trips to visit Great Aunt Elsie at Wisbech or Uncle Reginald Ward and his family in Ipswich.

Those without motor transport of their own were able to travel beyond the confines of Rollesby and Yarmouth on the many trips and outings organised by local individuals, clubs and private coach owners. Coaches were available for hire from many local firms to take villagers to special functions, sporting events and places of interest. Grandmother Miller organised numerous coach trips on behalf of the Ladies' Club, often day-long outings to Cromer or Hunstanton and evening trips to the theatre in Norwich or Great Yarmouth. As special events organiser for the Happy Rollers Club, Aunt Doris Miller was responsible for planning the club's

Rollesby Sunday School outing to Gorleston beach, 1951. Summertime coach trips and outings were a feature of village entertainment in the 1950s. (Sheila Allen)

programme of activities, including the annual visit to the pantomime at Great Yarmouth and summer coach trips to Cromer and the north Norfolk coast. Every spring, my grandmother organised a day trip by coach to see the tulip and daffodil fields of south Lincolnshire, and to visit the town of Spalding. In all the Flegg villages both the church and Methodist chapels organised outings as a summer treat for their Sunday school children.

VILLAGE'S LARGEST OUTING

In four coaches more than 130 Sunday School children with their parents and friends had their annual outing on Monday. At Lowestoft the children spent some time on the beach and the amusements while their parents went shopping. The party had lunch and tea at Lowestoft and in the evening went to Oulton Broad and while the children played in the park, the older members of the party went on the Broads. The Sunday School children's expenses were met from funds raised during the winter. Arrangements were made by Mrs H. Beck.

'Village News, Fleggburgh', *Yarmouth Mercury*, 23 June 1950

Although their destinations might be different, most adult coach trips followed a traditional format. During the initial part of the tour, the passengers were sufficiently occupied with chatting and looking at the scenery not to need much entertainment.

For many villagers, a coach trip was a welcome change from their daily routine. Among the passengers on this senior citizens' outing was Rollesby's celebrated smallest man, Bob Parker. (Glenda Tooke/Maureen Turner)

Occasionally, competitions and prize draws were held to promote interest. Usually, the intention of the organiser was for the party to arrive at the destination (a stately home or seaside town) in time for lunch, after which there was time allowed for the travellers to amuse themselves, including having tea, before being picked up again. The return journey often involved a short scenic tour of the area with a convenient break at a local public house. The last leg home was always enlivened by a communal singsong of old musical favourites.

In the late 1950s, I was occasionally invited by Aunt Doris Miller to join the coach trips that she organised for the Happy Rollers Club to entertain the senior citizens with my ukulele and guitar playing. On one memorable trip, the return journey involved a stop at a wayside public house where I was invited to play my ukulele. That evening was an unforgettable experience. The facilities consisted of one small dark dusty room with a trap door in one corner leading to the cellar. Around the room were numerous tables, chairs and settles, many occupied by a dozen or more local residents. Beer was initially drawn from barrels in the cellar into large enamelled jugs before being served in glasses at the bar. The landlord was a thick-set jolly middle-aged man who made our party very welcome. The barmaid was a very tall, extremely good-looking woman in her late twenties wearing a short-sleeved dress that buttoned down the front from neck to hem. The top buttons were left undone to reveal an ample cleavage, while most of the lower buttons were missing, a few having been replaced by safety pins. As she moved, especially when collecting the jugs of beer from the cellar, she revealed more than a modest amount of suntanned leg and left her admiring public in no doubt that there was little else beneath her dress other than the bare essentials. Most of the men in our party, myself included, spent most of the evening gazing mesmerised at this handsome beer-serving Amazon. After I had sung my complete repertoire of George Formby songs, the landlord thanked me for my efforts and declared that it was now their turn to entertain. Immediately, an ancient weather-wizened man dressed in a khaki army greatcoat and brown floppy hat, produced a harmonica from his pocket and accompanied the landlord while he sang various traditional and local folksongs about fishing for herring and ploughing the soil. Eventually, he was replaced by a second man dressed in a striped shirt, brown trousers held up by a belt of binder twine, a red spotted handkerchief tied around his neck and black hobnailed boots, who danced jigs on a wooden board accompanied by the same harmonica player. Fortified by numerous jugs of beer, everyone enthusiastically joined in a communal singsong, supported by an inharmonious harmonica and ukulele accompaniment, until it was time to leave for home.

OLD FOLKS OUTING

On Thursday the Happy Rollers Club had their monthly meeting in the Village Hall. After tea, provided by the helpers, they were taken for a mystery drive by coach to stormy windswept Cromer. After a short break they continued along the coast road and watched the angry sea. Arriving at Happisburgh, the party spent a happy evening entertained by the Victoria skiffle group. The secretary, Mrs C.A. Miller, organised the outing.

'Village news, Rollesby', *Yarmouth Mercury*, 8 July 1960

GOING ON VACATION

'Here comes summer', Jerry Keller, 1959

Until my time at university, I had never had a conventional holiday at a recognised holiday destination. The two occasions during my childhood when I had stayed away from home with my parents were simply visits to relatives – to Birmingham to celebrate the ending of the Second World War in 1945, and to Bexley Heath in Kent for Christmas 1950, a change from our usual Christmas arrangements as my grandmother was convalescing after an operation. Every year my father took the equivalent of two weeks leave from bricklaying, but only as odd days added on to the Christmas and August bank holidays, which he spent at home. He saved the remainder of his holiday allocation for use in times of bad weather during the winter months when he was unable to work outside. As a self-employed bricklayer, time off from work was unpaid, leaving him with little spare money for expensive family holidays away from home. Few of my relatives took holidays during the 1950s, other than time that they spent visiting their family or friends. Aunt Doris Miller travelled once a year to stay with her relatives at Chatham in Kent while Uncle Cecil Miller remained at home to manage the post office and grocery store in her absence. My Kent and Birmingham uncles and their families were lucky, as they could combine a visit to their parental homes in Rollesby and Great Yarmouth with a conventional holiday at the seaside or on the Broads. My parents and I were content just to stay at home and make use of the facilities available in our local neighbourhood.

My Miller grandparents did take an occasional one-week summer holiday, when they stayed in a chalet bungalow beside the beach at Hemsby, a mere 5 miles away from their home in Rollesby. Hemsby is a small coastal village 6 miles north of Great Yarmouth and, in the 1950s, was a popular seaside destination for local day-trippers as well as for many summer holidaymakers, mostly factory workers from the Midlands. The main village lay about a mile away from the beach around a stone-built church (flint-decorated in the traditional East Anglian style), with a station on the Midland and Great Northern Railway providing a convenient rail link with Birmingham and other Midland towns. The beach at Hemsby lay between the sea and two parallel rows of marram and fern-covered sand dunes. Between the dunes was a depression, known locally as 'The Valley', along which cars travelled on a track made from meshed metal rods laid on top of the sand. On either side of the valley were numerous small wooden bungalows that provided basic self-catering

The Valley, Hemsby. Hemsby was a popular holiday destination for locals as well as visitors from London and the Midlands, spending their vacation self-catering in the numerous wooden bungalows along the Valley. (Author's Collection)

The Enterprise Stores, Hemsby, where Tim's parents made a living by selling groceries and beach goods to residents and visitors staying in the beach chalets along the Valley Road. (Andrew Fakes)

accommodation for summer holidaymakers. From the station, a narrow lane (Beach Road) flanked on either side by two holiday camps (Maddieson's and Seacroft), led to a large cut through the sand dunes that gave easy access to the valley and the beach – a cut known as 'The Hemsby Gap'. At the head of the gap was a large black and white public house called The Lacon's Arms, and on either side of the access onto the beach were a number of wooden huts, one with an ornamental veranda, where their owners sold teas, ice creams, beach goods and holiday souvenirs. In my youth, I spent many hours on Hemsby beach with my cousins and friends sunbathing, building sand castles, playing ball, collecting seashells and paddling in the freezing North Sea. In my late teens, I regularly cycled to Newport, a district on the southern edge of Hemsby, to visit my friend Tim who lived at The Enterprise Stores, a shop adjacent to the valley where his parents (Arthur and Daisy Fakes) supplied groceries, newspapers and beach goods to village residents and summer visitors. Tim's local contacts made it possible for some of the wooden bungalows along the valley to be used in the quiet winter months as a venue for many noisy teenage parties. The lack of any form of heating in these bungalows was never seen as a deterrent in cold weather, as there were many diverse ways by which the teenage partygoers successfully contrived to keep warm.

My one and only proper seaside holiday ended in disaster almost before it had begun. In August 1951, my Miller grandparents invited Richard and me to join them on their weeklong summer break at Hemsby. The accommodation was a small wooden bungalow close to the gap, consisting of one large living room furnished

Grandmother Miller and the author on holiday at Hemsby, 1951. A few hours after this photograph was taken, I became ill with a severe bout of food poisoning. (Author's Collection)

with a miscellaneous collection of tables, chairs and unusable ornaments. Leading off from the living area was a galley kitchen and two bedrooms, one with a double bunk bed which was allocated to Richard and me. Clean water was obtained from a communal tap close to the bungalow, which was shared with a number of other holiday residences. An overhead electric cable provided power to the kitchen and for lighting. The only lavatory was a small and extremely smelly chemical toilet located in a hut to the rear of the building. Richard and I spent our first day at Hemsby exploring the beach and the dunes, and consuming numerous ice creams, candy flosses, cakes and other confectionary. After tea, I became violently ill with sickness and diarrhoea, and was hurriedly transported home by my worried grandparents. Instead of spending a week on holiday in Hemsby, I was confined to bed with what was undoubtedly a bad case of food poisoning. Luckily no-one else suffered from the illness, but I was extremely annoyed when Richard visited me, still in my sick bed, to say that he had remained with my grandparents for the whole of the week and had thoroughly enjoyed the experience.

YARMOUTH PEOPLE DO NOT HOLIDAY AT THE SEASIDE.
BUNGALOW HOLIDAYS

The difficulty of travelling far with children and babies has popularised the bungalow holiday. Hemsby, Scratby, Caister and a dozen other villages along the coast north and south of Yarmouth are fringed with bungalows to which Yarmouth families migrate in hot weather. This is as established a feature of Norfolk life as the exodus of Anglo-Indian families to the hills in India. Although many holiday camps are within easy distance of the town, organised relaxation en masse is not popular here except with teenagers who favour camps further north and well away from home. Members of youth movements and cycling clubs are the most ambitious Yarmouth holidaymakers because they feel it is cheaper and safer to travel abroad in groups. But the general attitude of the townspeople towards holidays seems to be summed up by an old lady who had never been further than Ormesby. 'I don't see no point in frittering money on trains and that when you've got the sea and everything ready for you here', she said.

Yarmouth Mercury, 11 February 1949

Cousins Margaret and Val with family members in front of their Gorleston snack bar.
Most of my cousins were expected to work during their summer holidays, not only to earn
extra pocket money but also to help their parents in busy times. (Val and Gem Cole)

Like many of my friends, the summer vacation from school and university provided me with an opportunity to supplement my personal finances by working part-time in the harvest or at nearby holiday resorts. At various times in my teens I picked blackcurrants and runner beans, lifted potatoes out from the ground, stooked sheaves of corn and drove corn-laden carts to the stack yard. I sold paperback books and saucy postcards on Yarmouth's Regent Road, served coffee and hotdogs in a seafront café, and prepared meals in the kitchens of Caister Holiday Camp. My summertime relaxation consisted solely of playing cricket at weekends, attending functions in the evening and the occasional day out. However, the longer university summer break did enable me to spend time away when the local holiday season ended in September.

At university I discovered hitchhiking, which, in the 1950s, was a cheap and easy way of travelling around the country, much favoured by students and National Servicemen. Personal safety seemed not to be an issue in those days, and many of

The author hitchhiking on the continent. Hitchhiking was a cheap and convenient way of travelling for cash-strapped students. My kitbag and guitar went everywhere with me.
(Author's Collection

my female student friends also hitchhiked, although they usually travelled in pairs as a safeguard against amorous drivers. With my possessions contained in an old army kitbag, I regularly thumbed lifts from Leicester to Rollesby, especially when my laundry needed doing or I felt in need of a good meal. During my university years I spent many September days hitchhiking to visit student friends in England and on the continent, staying overnight at youth hostels as I travelled. Sometimes alone and occasionally with a companion, I visited student friends in Holland, Belgium, Denmark, Germany and Austria. In those countries, hitchhiking was considered to be a suitably character-building activity and was encouraged among their young people. I frequently joined a long queue of young hitchhikers waiting for lifts at the entrance to various European autobahns, with a flag tied to our bags to indicate our country of origin and waving a hand-held sign stating our proposed destination. Occasionally things did not turn out as expected. On my first trip overseas, I embarked at Dunkirk to discover that I had arrived on a national bank holiday and, so, the roads were deserted. On a later trip, I realised too late that some countries did not welcome foreign hitchhikers. With a companion, I arrived at Malmö in Sweden to find that the youth hostel had closed and that nobody gave lifts to hikers. Having trudged 10 miles from the town along the coastal road, my friend and I were forced to spend an uncomfortable night sleeping in a pine forest before retracing our steps back to Malmö for a quick return to friendly Denmark.

THUMBS UP

Hitchhiking is a hobby peculiarly suited to the student. It satisfies two vital needs in his nature, the need to get something for nothing and the need to get it from as many people as possible.

Ripple, Leicester University, 14 November 1960

BANK HOLIDAYS

'Christmas Alphabet', Dickie Valentine, 1955

Annual holidays for my parents consisted merely of a few days break from work added onto the August, Christmas and New Year bank holidays, which they normally spent at home. Traditionally on August bank holiday Monday, we joined the queues of traffic to make our way along the Caister Road into Great Yarmouth for my father's once-yearly walk along Regent Road and the seafront Promenade. Even in the poorest of weathers, Yarmouth was crowded on bank holiday Monday with many day-trippers arriving on special excursion trains from London and the Midlands. Every year without fail, my father ate soft ice cream in a wafer bought from Vettese's Milk Bar and Ice Cream Parlour at the seafront end of Regent Road, and paid for us all to be weighed on a set of well-polished jockey's weighing scales located close to the entrance gates of the Britannia Pier.

We had no bathroom scales at home, so to be weighed accurately was a treat and sometimes a shock. (© Eastern Daily Press, 2007)

CROWDS ENJOYED THE ELUSIVE SUN

In spite of discouraging weather forecasts, day-trippers began pouring into the town by road and rail at an early hour on Monday, and by mid-morning the beaches and seafront were crowded with holidaymakers determined to enjoy themselves.

Shortly before noon the crowds on Regent Road were so dense that it took 20 minutes to walk from the Regal to the Marine Parade, and motorists were obliged to drive at a snail's pace because so many people were overflowing onto the roadway. For most of the day, cars and motorcycles were packed so close together along both sides of the seafront that people on foot sometimes had difficulty in finding a gap through which to cross the road, and neighbouring side streets were equally close packed with cars.

Yarmouth Mercury, 10 August 1956

NOTE THE DATES OF THE

GREAT YARMOUTH RACES, 1955
(Under Jockey Club Rules)

Wednesday & Thursday, 6th and 7th July   Wednesday & Thursday, 3rd and 4th August.
Tuesday, Wednesday & Thursday, 13th, 14th and 15th September

First Race each day 2.30 p.m   Six Races each day   Popular charges for admission
Refreshments obtainable on the course   Large Car Park adjoining the course
Public 'Bus service to the course   Running Commentary Broadcast over course
A " Family Car Parties " Enclosure—opened this year

My father's favourite summer treat was to spend Wednesday and Thursday afternoons at the August bank holiday flat race meeting at Great Yarmouth's North Denes racecourse. Mother and I usually accompanied him to one of the meetings but we did not have sufficient enthusiasm for horse racing to join him at both. The municipally owned seaside racecourse, constructed in 1920 to replace an older course on the South Denes, consisted of a large oval racetrack located between Yarmouth and Caister on sandy ground that it shared with the Caister links golf course. Normally, we arrived well before the start of racing and established a base for ourselves in the popular enclosures near to the centre of the course, where we had a picnic lunch and passed away the time before racing commenced by sunbathing and playing games. Various stalls sold teas and other refreshments, and, for the younger visitor, there was always a small but noisy fairground. At the start of racing, my father jostled his way through the crowds to take up a viewing position opposite to the main stand and as close to the winning post as possible. Race days, especially in fine sunny weather, were colourful occasions and there was always something to watch – the horses on parade with their jockeys dressed in bright racing silks, the hand-waving antics of the lines of bookmakers at their stands and the flashily dressed tipsters who tried eloquently to persuade punters to part with a shilling for the name of a sure and certain winner. My father was convinced that on one occasion he had been given an excellent tip by Prince Monolulu, a black tipster who normally sported a trademark ostrich-feathered headdress and who always famously declared 'Igottahorse'.

My favourite holiday was at Christmas. My father always took the days between Christmas and New Year as part of his annual leave – days which we enjoyed together as a family. Even for a spotty teenager who had long since discovered the truth about Santa Claus, Christmas was not only special but different from the rest of the year. For fifty-one weeks we lived every day in our small back sitting room, but at Christmas we moved into the front. For most of the year our front room was only occasionally used for special events and for family parties, but at Christmas we lived in it from Christmas Eve to New Year's Day, when we took down the decorations and moved back into the sitting room. For the week before Christmas, mother lit fires in the front room to warm it up before we assumed occupation, and home-made crêpe paper decorations were strung from various points along the picture rail to the central light fitting, both well-punctured by numerous pinholes, the legacy of many Christmases past.

Without the intrusive advertising of commercial television, Christmas in 1950s Norfolk persisted as a joyous religious festival and a family orientated occasion. Even the local newspapers restrained from promoting Christmas gifts and products until the beginning of December. Nevertheless, in Great Yarmouth the first recognised event of the Christmas season was the arrival, in early November, of Father Christmas at Arnold's annual fairy grotto, an event that was quickly followed by the appearance of elaborate festive shop window decorations and illuminated snowflakes hung from the streetlamps around the market square. Every December in the Regent Arcade, Sylvia the Florist produced a Christmas window display made entirely from flowers. Every year, the Rotary Club of Great Yarmouth presented the

Preparing the Christmas tree at Rollesby School, 1950. Decorations were simple yet Christmas in the 1950s was magic even to a rebellious teenager.
(Stephanie and Barry Gallant)

town with a Christmas tree, which was placed in a prominent position at the end of the market in front of the bomb-damaged St Nicholas Church and decorated with coloured lights. By tradition, at the annual carol service around the tree the congregation donated presents which the Rotary Club distributed among the needy of Great Yarmouth. Many of the Flegg villages retained charities based on rents from allotments of land allocated to the poor during the period of enclosure or legacies from former wealthy residents. Distributions from these charities also occurred around Christmas time. In Rollesby one charity took the form of gifts of coal allotted to eligible elderly residents, in Fleggburgh loaves of bread were given to all the children of the village and at Martham, boots and shoes were once provided for all the pupils attending the village school.

A Woman Looks Round – by Flapjack

Since Mr A.J. Osborne has been designing children's Christmas shows at Arnolds store over 600,000 people, children and adults, have wandered through the fairylands and wonderlands which he has created. Last Friday, the latest of Mr Osborne's creations 'Jenny's Christmas Dream' was opened by Father Christmas. This year's show is as colourful as ever. Fluorescent paint and water have been used very effectively and it should delight children of all ages who will wander along the dimly lighted passages in the weeks until Christmas. The show's façade is of Jenny's pretty little cottage. The theme is Jenny's journeys through fairyland in her dreams until she eventually wakes up and is greeted by Father Christmas in his castle. As you enter you see Jenny asleep and the final snow covered scene is of a castle with a fairy coach drawn by lifelike white rabbits and with cherubs pealing the Christmas bells. As usual there are two prices of admission – with or without presents.

Yarmouth Mercury, 7 November 1952

It was inevitable that Christmas events dominated our leisure time during December and early January. At home we wrote out our Christmas cards, often inserting a handwritten letter to a distant relative or friend inside the card, and made decorations and streamers from strips of coloured crêpe paper. Mother made a Christmas cake, a rich fruitcake that she covered with marzipan and thick white royal icing. Every year my father brought home a small fir tree which we decorated with tinsel, Christmas ornaments and candles, and placed in the bay window of our front room. Every year after Christmas, he planted the tree in our garden in the hope that it might survive until the next December. Every year without fail it died. Well-attended Christmas whist drives, dances and socials were held in many of the local village halls, and Nativity plays and carol services were held at St George's Church and the Methodist chapel. The weeks before Christmas were very busy for my Uncle Cecil Miller at the post office, sorting and delivering the Christmas mail. At Christmastime, mother was usually employed part-time as a relief postman helping with the two daily deliveries around the village. In my late teens I took over from my mother as the Christmas relief postman. Although it was hard work, this was a job

St George's Church Nativity play, 1952. Every year, members of both the church and chapel in Rollesby performed a nativity play, sang carols around the village and organised a Christmas party for their Sunday school children. (Stephanie and Barry Gallant)

envied by my friends because, on the final delivery day, almost everyone in the village gave me a Christmas box, a mince pie and a glass of sherry, providing a suitable kick-start to my Christmas celebrations.

But most of all Christmas was a time for parties, normally children's and family parties, however, in our late teens, my friends and I preferred to celebrate Christmas at the many village dances and special Christmas Balls held in Great Yarmouth, usually with a large bunch of mistletoe to spice up the occasion. Nevertheless, many of Great Yarmouth's larger firms not only provided dinner-dances for their employees but also organised Christmas parties for their employees' children. In 1952, my father took temporary employment with H.A. Holmes & Son, a large building firm based in Great Yarmouth. Despite some reservations on my part, being almost a teenager, I joined nearly 200 children of all ages at the Gorleston Football Social Club for a Christmas tea, followed by an evening's entertainment which included a Punch & Judy show, a conjurer, various games, communal singing and a present for everyone distributed by an unconvincing Father Christmas with an ill-fitting beard. As well as the regular Nativity play at Christmas, both the church and the chapel gave a party as a treat for their Sunday school children. My cousin Stephanie held a Christmas party every year for her friends and cousins well into her teenage years. As her guests got older, Postman's Knock and other similar party games gained an added significance. Unfortunately for me, my partner in many of these games often turned out to be one of my aunts.

SUNDAY SCHOOL PARTY

The Methodist Sunday School held its annual party last Thursday. Each child received a box of sweets, a bag of nuts, a cracker and a prize from the Christmas tree. Bernard Wymer received a prize for 100 per cent attendance for the third successive year.

'Village news, Rollesby', *Yarmouth Mercury*, 8 January 1954

Over the Christmas period, family parties were the norm. We spent Christmas Day with my Miller grandparents in their small house at Hall Cottages, together with at least a dozen other Miller relatives. After my grandmother died in 1957, Aunt Doris Miller at the post office took over the mantle of Christmas Day hostess. The day consisted mainly of exchanging presents, eating (Christmas dinner at 12.30 p.m. and a large tea at 5 p.m.), sleeping and playing games. On Boxing Day, the party was repeated at our house, with some of our Cole relatives adding to the numbers. The Millers were not heavy drinkers, most of them preferring lemonade or squash with their meals and a small glass or two of sherry or port to liven up the evening. My uncles enjoyed an occasional tot of whisky but my father was satisfied with a small glass of cider. My father drank very little alcohol as he reacted badly to it, and insisted that anyone consuming more than two drinks in an evening was an alcoholic and a blot on society. Once I was eighteen, a bottle of beer was also included on the drinks table as I was not particularly fond of sherry or port. New drinks were sometimes tried with great ceremony. Mother introduced everyone to Snowballs, a frothy mixture of Advocaat, lime and lemonade, which she insisted was called Egg Flip. One year, Uncle George Miller brought a bottle of homemade potato wine, which only Grandma Cole bravely tried. The cork was then replaced in the bottle and reopened the following year for Grandma Cole to try again, as she insisted that she had enjoyed her first taste. How the wine survived I do not know, but the effect was dramatic as Grandma Cole was eventually put to bed with a bad headache. Grandmother Miller's preference was Stone's Ginger wine, while Grandfather Miller stuck to Wincarnis, a tonic wine for the elderly. Clearly, we had little experience or understanding of wine other than champagne, which was drunk on very rare and special occasions, and port and sherry.

My introduction to wine occurred at university and then only as a cheap drink to take to parties when I was unable to afford my preferred Party Fours or Sevens (four or seven pints of Watney's Red Barrel beer in a metal can which was opened by punching two holes on either side of the can's top with a triangular-shaped key). On arrival at a party, bottles of sweet Sauternes, Liebfraumilch or Mateus Rosé were presented to the party host, which were then often poured into a large bowl, mixed with a tin of fruit, fortified with a spirit or cider, and served as a punch. At the end of my first term at university, I was invited to a party given by the Professor of Philosophy for all students attending one of his courses. The food was excellent but I was surprised to find that the only drink available was either red or white wine, which we all consumed in large quantities. The party ended abruptly around midnight when a lecturer's wife was sick, fouling the kitchen with a half-digested mixture of potato mayonnaise and red wine. From that day onwards I have never been able to drink large quantities of wine without feeling ill.

Other than for the Queen's speech, an event never missed, listening to the radio or watching television was banned at Christmas. The time between and after meals was always filled with conversation and games. In the afternoon of Christmas Day, the children played with their new toys or read books, the ladies chatted before setting out the tea and the men played cards or poker dice. The evening was a continuous round of singing, dancing, charades and playing cards and games, usually for prizes. Mother always organised 'The Memory Test', a game in which a hundred or more small objects were circulated among the players who, after all the objects had been seen, were each in turn given any object that they could remember. The player with the most objects at the end of the game was the winner. I enjoyed 'Mother Mackenzie's Dead', a rather gruesome memory game much enjoyed by the younger family members where, in turn, each player had to add a reason why she died, after recalling all the reasons given by previous players. Anyone forgetting or omitting a previous reason was knocked out of the game. 'Mother Mackenzie's dead', 'What did she die of?', 'A broken leg', 'A broken leg and diarrhoea', 'A broken leg, diarrhoea and the scurvy', and so on, creating an immense list of ailments suffered by poor Mother Mackenzie, to the amusement of the players. Game followed game (musical chairs, pass-the-parcel, ring-on-a-string, spin-the-wheel, hunt-the-thimble, to name but a few) until about 10.30 p.m. when we had supper and went home exhausted.

11

The Summer Season

EAST COAST SEASIDE HOLIDAYS

'Yellow polka dot bikini', Brian Hyland, 1960

From the end of May until the beginning of September, the Norfolk seaside holiday season provided many additional attractions to liven up my leisure time. In my early teens, it was the sun, sand and sea, the amusement arcades in Great Yarmouth and the many other activities associated with a traditional British seaside holiday resort. In my late teens, it was the gangs of giggling girls that were gathered around the numerous seafront jukeboxes singing to loud rock 'n' roll music, sitting in the many smoke-filled coffee bars or just parading around the fairground at the Pleasure Beach, seeking the thrill of a holiday romance.

Every Saturday throughout the summer, thousands of holidaymakers from London and the Midlands arrived at Great Yarmouth and the smaller resorts nearby for a week or a fortnight by the sea. In some of the weeks during the summer season, the majority of the visitors were mainly from a single city such as Leicester, when all the schools and factories of that city closed at the same time for the workers and their families to take an annual paid holiday entitlement en masse, in other weeks they were from Nottingham, Derby, Coventry or Birmingham as, in turn, their manufacturing also shut down. At the beginning and end of the season there were weeks designated specifically for entertaining the handicapped and the elderly.

In the early 1950s, holidaymakers mostly arrived by specially organised trains at Yarmouth's three railway stations – Vauxhall, Southtown and Beach. By the late 1950s, many more arrived by coach, car or motorcycle forming long queues into the town, especially along the A47, the Acle New Road. Every Saturday, gangs of small boys, equipped with box-carts, prams and wheelbarrows, congregated outside the various rail and coach stations, offering to carry the visitors' bags and suitcases to their holiday accommodation for sixpence or one shilling. In the early 1950s, most of the holidaymakers preferred to take half-board or bed & breakfast in the small hotels and private guesthouses of Great Yarmouth. Many returned every year to the same holiday address and established a lifetime friendship with their seaside landlady. Some holidaymakers enjoyed the organised chaos of a holiday camp or camping in tents on the racecourse. By the late 1950s, large chalet and caravan parks had been added on the North and South Denes to cater for the growing number of summer visitors, especially those that arrived by car. Wealthier holidaymakers, including the

Holidaymakers arriving at Yarmouth's Vauxhall station, 1953.
(© Eastern Daily Press 2007)

stars of the summer variety shows, stayed at the bigger hotels, especially at the Carlton, Yarmouth's premier hotel opposite the Wellington Pier, where afternoon tea-takers were serenaded by a pianist on a grand piano. The 1950s were certainly the heyday of the East Coast seaside holiday industry, before cheap continental package holidays and the promise of uninterrupted sunshine became affordable by most people.

The 1950s were also a boom time for seaside holiday camps. Camps were established near to Great Yarmouth at Caister, Hemsby, Gorleston and Hopton, and proved a popular attraction to young people and families with children. Established in 1906 by a socialist visionary, Fletcher Dodd, and one of the first of its kind in the country, Caister Holiday Camp occupied a hilltop site between the Caister water tower and the beach, bisected by the then main A149 from Caister village to Ormesby, a mile or so distant. Basic living and sleeping accommodation was provided by row upon row of wooden chalets, and all meals were served at specified times in large communal dining rooms. In the small coastal village of Hemsby, two similar holiday camps – Maddieson's Hemsby Holiday Camp (which was established in 1920) and the smaller family-owned Seacroft Holiday Camp (opened in 1930) – provided weekly seaside accommodation for over one thousand visitors. By the 1950s, ten or more holiday camps had been established along the coast within 10 miles of Great Yarmouth, including the Gorleston Super Holiday Camp and at least five campsites in the seaside village of Hopton. As well as being within easy reach of the beach, all of the camps provided day-long entertainment for their visitors. In each camp's main hall, dances and cabaret entertainment took place continuously throughout the day, and competitions, both the serious and the not so serious, were held on their sports fields: tug-of-war, knobbly knees, bathing beauty and beautiful baby competitions, to name but a few. Cricket and football matches, three-legged, wheelbarrow, sack and egg-and-spoon races, as well as proper competitive sprints, were all supported enthusiastically by everyone, young and old, intent on having a good time. Swimming competitions were held in their pools and in the various sports halls, art classes, whist drives, and games of darts, table tennis, billiards and snooker, provided entertainment even in the wettest of weather. In the evening, the adults relaxed in the bars, danced or attended the camp's variety shows, while chalet walkers listened for restless youngsters, recalling their parents through

Holidaymakers at Seacroft Holiday Camp, 1950. During the 1950s, a dozen or more local camps provided inexpensive holidays for visitors, mainly from the Midlands. (Andrew Fakes)

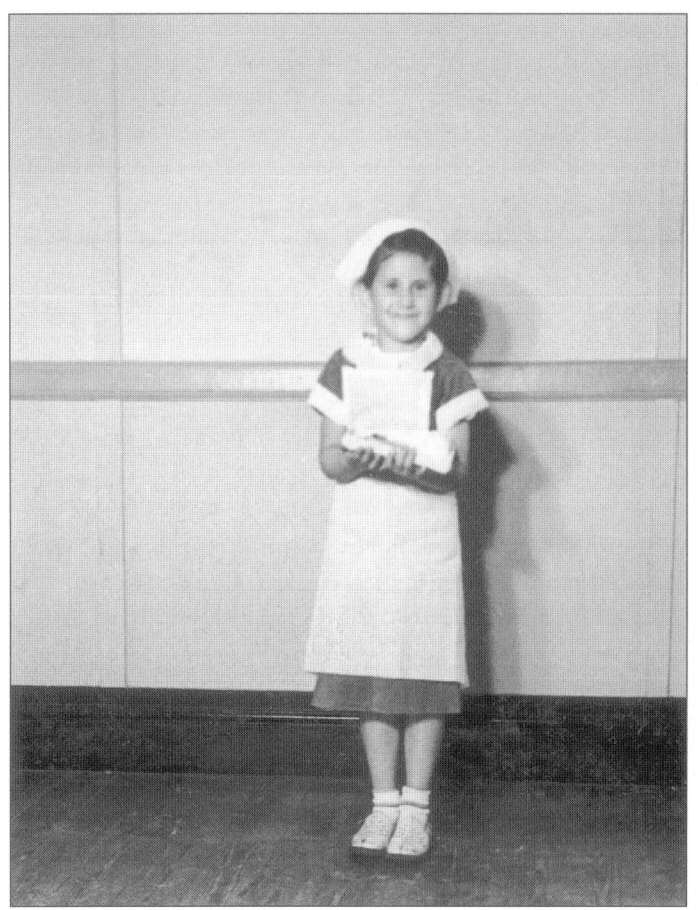

My future wife, aged seven, dressed as a 'Norman Hartnell Nurse' for a fancy dress competition at Hopton's Constitutional Holiday Camp in 1950. Living in Leicester meant that her family holidays were usually taken at an East Coast seaside resort. (Author's Collection)

the inter-camp tannoy systems if their presence was felt necessary. For the adventurous, the surrounding countryside could be explored on unusual cycles made for two or more, Heath Robinson contraptions resembling benches on wheels.

For the local population, the holiday camps provided the chance of relatively well-paid employment during the summer months. My mother and Aunt Edith worked at various times as Saturday morning chalet cleaners, and I spent my last summer break before leaving for university preparing food in the kitchens of Caister Holiday Camp. As an employee, there were many opportunities to use the recreational facilities of the camp and to gain access to young female holidaymakers. However, it soon became clear to me that the kitchen staff were less attractive to the better-looking female holidaymakers than the entertainments staff, Caister Holiday Camp's equivalent to the Butlins' redcoats. This impression was confirmed on my nineteenth birthday when I had arranged to meet a young lady in the camp's bar before taking her to the regular nightly dance in the main hall. I arrived at the bar a full half-hour before the designated time to meet my date, hopefully anticipating a birthday conquest, only to be told by a mutual acquaintance that she had stood me up in favour of the camp's P.E. instructor.

Cleaners at Caister Holiday Camp. Mother (extreme right) and her friends cleaned chalets every Saturday morning. (Author's Collection)

NORFOLK'S GOLDEN SANDS

'Beyond the sea', Bobby Darin, 1960

The long sandy beaches of the east Norfolk coast were a great attraction to locals and holidaymakers alike. Once the coast had been cleared of mines and other hazards placed there as a defence against invasion during the war, I spent many summer days on the sands with my friends and family. I often cycled to Hemsby and Horsey with a packed lunch hanging from my handlebars. Horsey was a particular favourite for me as the receding tides often left small lagoons of water called 'the shallows', which were ideal for swimmers lacking in confidence. At Great Yarmouth, the stretch of beach between the Britannia and Wellington Piers was cleared by army sappers and German prisoners of war in time for the 1946 summer season. The gap in the Britannia Pier created during the hostilities was repaired and the remaining beaches cleared in 1947, completing a post-war return to summertime normality.

During my summer holidays, I spent many hours on the beach at Yarmouth, sometimes alone, occasionally with friends, watching the antics of the visiting holidaymakers and, in my later teens, making eyes at the many groups of teenage girls sunbathing on the sands, usually with little success. Unlike many of my friends, I disliked sunbathing in company and steadfastly refused to remove my shirt in the presence of females. As a small child, I had suffered from a bad bout of whooping cough which had caused a deformation of my ribcage – a deformity I considered so obvious and ugly that, as a teenager, I was convinced it marred my physical appearance and would prove to be a deterrent to potential female partners.

During the 1950s, Great Yarmouth was so popular with visitors as a holiday destination that, on sunny days in the mid-summer months of July and August, the central beach between the two piers was usually filled with groups of holidaymakers. Some sat around a blanket that was laid on the sand, others on deckchairs that they hired for the day from an attendant on the promenade, frequently positioned in the

Holidaymakers on Central Beach close to the old jetty. Suits, jackets, hats and ties were normal beachwear in 1955. (© Eastern Daily Press 2007)

lee of a canvas windbreak that protected their site from wind-blown sand. Fathers (dressed in their best suits, flat caps or trilby hats, with their shirtsleeves rolled up military style), mothers (wearing loose floral dresses displaying peeling sunburnt arms and chests), teenagers and children (in shorts and one-piece bathing costumes) vied for the best position close to the sea. Early risers were rewarded by the best sites on the beach, while latecomers had to be satisfied with a seat on the promenade or a space on the lawns in the roadside gardens along Marine Parade. Frequently, family groups were so closely packed that walkers had to pick their way carefully through the crowds, trying hard not to kick sand over the sunbathers strewn across the ground. Movement was so restricted that activities were limited to sleeping, reading, digging holes in the sand, burying siblings, making sandcastles and paddling in the sea. Those wanting to play more energetic ball games or fly kites in the wind had to seek the emptier spaces of the north shore beyond the Britannia Pier. Courting couples sought privacy away from prying eyes in the shadows under the two main piers or the sand dunes on the far north beach.

Refreshments, beach goods and postcards were sold at numerous wooden teashops erected along the beachside promenade, their interior tables and chairs providing a convenient shelter in the event of rain. Individual traders toured the beaches selling ice creams, kites, plastic windmills on a stick, and tin buckets and spades from trays hung around their necks. Children and adults frequently staggered back from the teashops carrying fistfuls of melting ice cream cornets and pink candyflosses on a stick. Entertainment was provided by a Punch & Judy show near to the Britannia Pier, where numerous small children sat on the sand in thrall to the villainous Punch, shrieking loudly at every appearance of the hungry crocodile. Between shows, a large clock pinned to the front of the canvas kiosk indicated the time of the next performance. Adjacent to the Punch & Judy show, adults threw pennies into a bucket in appreciation of the sand sculptures created by the Yarmouth beach artist, Fred Bultitude, often realistic depictions of wounded soldiers and dead horses. All along the water's edge, inshore fishermen attempted to augment their income by offering holidaymakers boat trips out to sea to observe the seals on Scroby Sands. After dark, the beach became the territory of the young, as couples walked hand-in-hand along the moonlit shoreline. My friends and I often accompanied groups of teenage girls along the seashore from the Pleasure Beach back to their caravans on the North Denes, occasionally pausing for a while in the shelters along the promenade.

GREAT YARMOUTH'S GOLDEN MILE

'Love letters in the sand', Pat Boone, 1957

Apart from the beach, the main attractions for Yarmouth's visitors lay along Regent Road (linking the shopping centre around the market square with the seafront) and Marine Parade (running adjacent to and parallel with the beach from the North Denes towards the harbour's mouth). In the summer, both roads were packed with pedestrians and traffic, but in the winter they were frequently deserted with many of their shops, coffee bars and restaurants closed and boarded up. A visit to the Empire cinema on the seafront during the winter months often involved braving torrential rain and gale force winds driving in from the sea. Wind-blown sand gathered inside the empty shelters on the Promenade and covered the pavements and gardens along Marine Parade. Like many Yarmouthians, I enjoyed the bracing nature of walking on a deserted seafront in winter almost as much as the glamour of the beach in summer.

In the 1950s, Regent Road stretched uninterrupted from the Regal cinema on Theatre Plain towards the seafront, intersecting Marine Parade close to the Royal Aquarium. On either side of the road, cafés, restaurants, gift shops and public houses catered for the immediate needs of summer holidaymakers. Entertainment was also provided by a second cinema, the Regent, two billiard saloons and a waxworks exhibition. In the summer, live variety shows were staged at the Regal in place of the regular films. There were also branches of Woolworth and British Home Stores, a large garage and a Roman Catholic church. I regularly travelled along Regent Road, often dallying by, and occasionally buying from, my three favourite shops: Docwra's Rock Shop, the Bloater King and Vettese's Milk Bar. At the Rock Shop, I often stood fascinated while watching the firm's employees rolling (or pulling) long sausages of pink candy seaside rock on a special table. At the start of the process, words were created using thick strips of red and white candy stuck together. This was then folded over to make a large cylinder, placed on the table and rolled out to form long thin strips of Yarmouth rock, which were then cut into standard lengths by a lady with a large pair of iron scissors. The sweet smell of candy pervaded the air and, inside the shop, visitors were able to buy not only sticks of rock but also sweets and humbugs in jars, lollipops and candy made into novelty shapes. On the opposite side of the road, holidaymakers purchased boxes of Yarmouth's world famous bloaters at the Bloater King to send to their friends by post. In the shop's bay window, a man sat all day long nailing the lids onto boxes of bloaters with a machine. Close to the junction of Regent Road with Marine Parade was Vettese's Milk Bar, which, as I recall, was the first in Yarmouth to introduce soft ice cream dispensed from a machine. My parents and I were addicted to Vettese's and, on visits to the seaside at Great Yarmouth, never failed to enjoy not only cones and wafers of their soft ice cream but also colourful Knickerbocker Glories, banana splits, fruit sundaes and my favourite ice cream sodas, which I drank through a straw.

At the age of fifteen, I was employed in the summer by Uncle Bob Cole to sell cheap paperback novels and saucy postcards on a courtyard site that he had rented in a prime position at the seaside end of Regent Road. Dressed in a white coat with a money pouch hung over my shoulder, I spent many hours during my school vacation encouraging holidaymakers to buy Hank Janson novels, comic books and risqué postcards. The venture was certainly a success as Uncle Bob was also able to purchase a small café in Gorleston where he ran a successful family business. Through Uncle Bob, I obtained summer employment for another year at a coffee bar on Regent Road called Alfredo's, where the proprietor tempted holidaymakers with the latest 1950s food craze, hot dogs, as well as coffee, teas and snacks. For most of that summer, my staple diet was hot dogs with onions and tomato sauce, washed down by ice cream sodas.

Nevertheless, the main holiday attractions lay along the Marine Parade, Great Yarmouth's Golden Mile, which stretched from the waterways near to the Royal Aquarium south to the Pleasure Beach fairground. To one side of the road were entrances to the Britannia and Wellington Piers, a roller-skating rink, an open-air saltwater swimming pool, the Marina and the Pleasure Beach, and, between these, numerous gardens, bowling greens and tennis courts. On the other side of the road, away from the beach, were numerous hotels, guesthouses, restaurants, public houses, museums and amusement arcades, the Windmill, Empire and Royal Aquarium cinemas and the Hippodrome Circus. Despite working part-time during most of my summer vacations, I was still able to make use of the many additional entertainment and leisure opportunities available to me by virtue of living close to this popular seaside holiday resort.

Among my mother's favourite venues was the Marina, a circular open-air amphitheatre where regular musical concerts were held, which was built in 1937 to replace an earlier concert arena called the Singer's Ring. Inside the Marina, the audience sat on rows of canvas chairs in front of a circular stage on which the musicians performed. Only the stage and a small strip around the edge of the Marina were covered with a roof, the latter supported every 10 yards or so by a circle of concrete pillars, providing the audience with some rudimentary cover in the event of

During the 1950s, various show bands performed at the popular Marina open-air auditorium on Great Yarmouth's seafront, including Ronnie Mills and his Orchestra and Harry Hudson's Melody Boys. (Author's Collection)

*Neville Bishop and his Wolves performed at the Marina in the late 1950s. Many young
visitors will remember with pleasure Uncle Neville's morning children's parties.*
(Author's Collection)

rain. In bad weather it was usual for the audience to get wet, as most of them
preferred to stay in their seats protected from the elements by umbrellas, hats and
raincoats. During the summer, concerts took place twice daily at 3 p.m. and 7.30 p.m.,
with talent and bathing beauty competitions held in between the music.
Competition heats were held each day during the week, culminating in a grand final
which took place at the Friday evening concert. In the 1950s, the resident bands at
the Marina were Ronnie Mills and his Orchestra (1949–51), Waldini and his
Orchestra (1952–3), Harry Hudson and his Melody Boys (1954) and the ever-
popular Neville Bishop's Showband (1955 onwards). The music played was mainly
light popular music and the audience was encouraged to join in and sing with the
band. In my early teens, I often accompanied my mother to afternoon performances,
usually on a Wednesday. In my late teens, I considered the music too old-fashioned
for a youth gripped with a craze for rock 'n' roll, although I did maintain a passing
interest in the bathing beauty competitions.

For most holidaymakers, the summer seaside variety shows were the prime
evening attraction and featured many well-known personalities from radio and
television. By the end of the 1950s, summer shows were held all along the Golden
Mile at theatres on the Wellington and Britannia Piers, the Royal Aquarium and the

Windmill, as well as at the Regal on Regent Road. In 1950, entertainment was confined to the theatres on the two piers but in 1954, when the Britannia Pier theatre was destroyed by fire, the Royal Aquarium and the Windmill ceased film shows during the summer in favour of live variety, although the Windmill continued to show cartoon films for children during the daytime. When a rebuilt Britannia Pier theatre reopened in 1959, Great Yarmouth offered no less than five live variety shows to its residents and visitors, all featuring a nationally known celebrity, usually a well-known comedian. At most of the venues the same show was performed throughout the summer season, but at the Regal Theatre shows changed on a weekly basis with a new starring performer every week. Most of the performances were a collection of unrelated acts, with the star celebrity featuring at the end of the first and second halves of the show. Shows usually began with a chorus line of a dozen or more scantily dressed ladies linked together arm-in-arm, dancing and kicking their legs in unison, can-can style, to the music of the pit orchestra. This was

Regal Theatre Programme for Lonnie Donegan, 1958.

1950	Britannia Pier	Laughing Thru	Frankie Howerd
	Wellington Pier	Showtime	Ray Barbour and Beryl Reid
1951	Britannia Pier	Meet The Stars	Ronnie Ronalde and Max Bygraves
	Wellington Pier	Showtime	Jack Storey and Max & Maisie Norris
1952	Britannia Pier	Good Evans	Norman Evans
	Wellington Pier	Showtime	Jack Storey
1953	Britannia Pier	Keep 'em Laughing	Jimmy Jewel and Ben Warriss
	Wellington Pier	Showtime	George Boulton
1954	Royal Aquarium	You Can't Help Laughing	Ted Ray
	Wellington Pier	Showtime	Don Arrol
1955	Royal Aquarium	You Can't Help Laughing	Charlie Chester and the Beverley Sisters
	Wellington Pier	The Ronnie Ronalde Show	Ronnie Ronalde
	Windmill	Tommy Trinder in Person	Tommy Trinder
1956	Royal Aquarium	The Laugh of a Lifetime	Jimmy Jewel and Ben Warriss
	Wellington Pier	The Ronnie Ronalde Show	Ronnie Ronalde
	Windmill	In the Grove	Eddie Calvert
1957	Royal Aquarium	Right Monkey	Al Read
	Wellington Pier	Light Up the Town	Benny Hill
	Windmill	If it's Laughter You're After	Tommy Trinder
1958	Royal Aquarium	Ace High	Vic Oliver, Pearl Carr & Teddy Johnson
	Wellington Pier	Light Up Again	Ruby Murray and Tommy Cooper
	Windmill	This is Your Laugh	Derek Roy
1959	Britannia Pier	Top of the Town	Nat Jackley, Stan Stennett & Joan Turner
	Royal Aquarium	The Lonnie Donegan Show	Lonnie Donegan
	Wellington Pier	The Big Show	David Nixon, Joan Regan and The King Brothers
	Windmill	The George Formby Show	George Formby
1960	Britannia Pier	Tops for Laughter	Jimmy Jewel and Ben Warriss
	Royal Aquarium	Pot Luck	Charlie Chester
	Wellington Pier	Showtime	Charlie Drake, Lenny the Lion and the Mudlarks
	Windmill	The Tommy Trinder Show	Tommy Trinder

Summer shows on the Golden Mile, Great Yarmouth, 1950–60.

followed in succession by various supporting performances of ten minutes each that included acrobats, jugglers, unicyclists, knife throwers, conjurers, solo singers and various other novelty acts, before ending with a thirty-minute performance given by the star of the show. Occasionally, one of the supporting speciality acts was so good that the star performer was a disappointment by comparison. I particularly loved the Egyptian sand dancing of Wilson, Keppel and Betty.

My parents enjoyed live variety and always made at least one annual visit to a summer show in Great Yarmouth, normally during my father's August bank holiday break from work. As a family group we enjoyed performances from well-known entertainers such as Norman Evans with his famous 'over the garden wall' act, the laid-back magic of Tommy Cooper, whistler Ronnie Ronalde, comedians Jimmy

A crowded Yarmouth seafront with the Marina and Britannia Pier in the background. Mother spent many hours in the Marina listening to the music of Neville Bishop and his Orchestra. (© Eastern Daily Press 2007)

Jewel and Ben Warriss, and singer comedian Stan Stennett, who had me in stitches with his song about three cowboys Art, Bart and Fargo, which he sang with a long emphasis on the 'F' of Fargo. My parents preferred traditional comedy acts and failed to share my enthusiasm for The Lonnie Donegan Show. Their preference was for shows that took place on one of the two piers, both of which extended well out into the sea in the 1950s. We always arrived at least an hour before the start of the show so that we could wander around the deck, enjoy the various amusements and stalls, and stare out to sea from the end of the pier. As a child, I always found it quite disconcerting to see the sea beneath my feet through gaps in the pier's planking.

Attached to the front of the Wellington Pier was a large glass conservatory known locally as 'The Winter Gardens', which had been purchased by Yarmouth Corporation and brought to Yarmouth in 1903 from its original location in Torquay. This was used in the summer as a venue for musical performances, tea and evening dances, but in the winter it became the home of the Great Yarmouth Roller-Skating Club. In 1949, an additional outdoor roller-skating rink, the largest in East Anglia, was opened in gardens adjacent to the pier and used by the club during the summer. Throughout the whole of the 1950s, roller-skating was a very popular and

Wonder Wheels roller-skating troupe, 1958.

relatively inexpensive pastime for young people. Ice skating had long been a tradition among the residents of Broadland Norfolk and the Fens – my father was a keen and skilful skater – but even in the hard winters of the late 1940s and early '50s, when the Broads regularly froze over, outdoor ice skating was limited to no more than two weeks in every year. Roller-skating, on the other hand, provided an opportunity for year-round sport. Many of my cousins were roller skaters and bought their skates at Doughty's Sports on Regent Road or Ward's on King Street, professional-looking skating boots with a toe stop that performed the function of a brake. I owned a pair of skates which I attached to the bottom of my shoes with leather straps but, despite much practice and many grazed knees, I could never master the skill of standing upright while travelling on eight small wheels.

Many interesting opportunities existed for those who could skate. The Roller-Skating Club was so well supported that it was able to employ professional skaters to give personal tuition to club members, well-known names such as Frank Martin and Jocelyn Taylor (1950–1), Howarth Hargreaves and Sheila Wilkinson (1952–5), Ted Norton and Sheilah Bate (1956), Ted Norton and Margaret Derbyshire (1957), Ken

Hookham and Margaret Derbyshire (1958), and George Thompson and Jocelyn Taylor (1959 onwards), all known skaters some of whom were national champions in their sport. Under their stewardship, the club gave regular well-attended skating shows in the summer, variously called Skaterscades, Wonder Wheels and Roller Revels. Every year, we joined an enthusiastic audience braving Norfolk's variable weather to sit around the rink in the open air and marvel at the skating skills of the club members, the synchronised dancing of the skating teams and the artistry of the professionals. Wednesday was exclusively club night but on other evenings during the week the rink was available to everybody. Similar facilities existed in Lowestoft and at the Rollerdrome in the grounds of the Gorleston Super Holiday Camp. Playing hockey on roller-skates was also very popular and local teams competed in the Norfolk and Suffolk Roller Hockey League.

WELLINGTON PIER
OUTDOOR ROLLER SKATING RINK

The Great Yarmouth
Roller Skating Club
Presents

WONDER

1958

WHEELS

Lucky No.
551

Programme **6d.**
(In Aid of Clubs Funds)

The Wonderettes junior roller-skating group, 1958. In their teens, cousins Francis and Val, and cousin-in-law Gem were all enthusiastic members of Yarmouth's roller-skating club. In the 1958 Wonder Wheels show, Gem gave an acrobatic performance with the club professional that amazed her friends and terrified her father. (Val and Gem Cole)

CLEVER SKATING BY 'ROLLER REVELS'

In spite of a cold wind and intermittent showers there was a large audience on the opening night to applaud the 14 items which included solos, pairs, chorus numbers and some entertaining 'skaterbatics' and fooling. Perhaps the most outstanding thing about the evening was the precision with which the skaters carried out their movements, circling around effortlessly, yet in that perfect order which indicated hours of careful rehearsal. Outstanding too were the costumes which were all made by relatives and friends of the cast. There was a big round of applause for Diana Holt whose solo turn 'Junior Miss' was a remarkably polished achievement for one so young. Another solo pair who attracted a lot of notice was Brian Colclough and Pat Steward, the reigning champions of the Roller Skating Club, who individually hold the men's figures and women's figures titles, and together the pairs title and the senior dance title. Laurie Brewer and Heather Nutman, another accomplished pair, also presented a skilful turn, as also did 'The Mascots', two tiny children who opened the show. Biggest round of applause of the evening was, however, deservedly left for the two professionals who performed two items as a pair and kept the audience spellbound by their grace and virtuosity. A solo number was also given by Sheila Wilkinson who, in 1953, was the professional figure skating champion of Great Britain. As a pair, Howarth Hargreaves and Sheila Wilkinson are the 1954 holders of the British professional dance skating championships. 'Krazee Comics' were contributed by Colin Brown and Tony Bean, and there was some accomplished acrobatics by Ray Wharwell and Cyril Edwards. The dance team who made their first appearance in a colourful medley 'Gold and Silver' also did some precision dancing and chorus numbers were performed by a troupe of girls.

Yarmouth Mercury, 18 June 1954

In my later teens, my main interest along the Golden Mile lay in the Pleasure Beach fairground and the numerous amusement arcades where the younger men and women, locals and holidaymakers, not only sought thrills on the rides and played the various penny slot machines, jukeboxes and pinball tables, but also vied to establish relationships with the opposite sex. The Botton brothers' Pleasure Beach was, and still is, located at the most southerly end of the Golden Mile and, in the 1950s, consisted of a long area of land between the road and the beach with fixed amusements along the edges, and roundabouts, dodgems and various switchback rides down the centre either side of a mat slide. At the far end of the fairground was the inappropriately named scenic railway, a roller coaster that was brought to Great Yarmouth from Paris in 1932 and was, at the time, one of the longest rides in the country. My first experience of this roller coaster was at the age of ten when I pestered my grandfather to take me on the 'little railway'. Eventually, my grandfather gave in to my wishes and we settled ourselves into one of the carriages. It soon became clear to me that the experience was not what I expected and I spent the duration of the ride fixed in silent terror with my teeth clenched firmly shut.

Enjoying the scenic railway at Great Yarmouth's Pleasure Beach, 1953. Clearly, health and safety were not burning issues in the 1950s. (© Eastern Daily Press 2007)

At the highest point of the ride, my grandfather's trilby hat blew off never to be found again and at the end of the ride I was sick. Despite a subsequent dislike of roller coasters, I frequently rode the Yarmouth scenic railway in an attempt to impress reluctant females.

Opposite the entrance of the Pleasure Beach was a large Galloper with three ranks of horses that rose and fell as the roundabout turned to a fairground organ accompaniment. Nearby were the dodgems, which were a convenient place for me and my companions of the day to loiter, leaning nonchalantly against its surrounding enclosure fence. Whenever two girls were spotted climbing into a dodgem car, one of my friends and I would climb into another and attempt to effect an introduction by continually ramming their vehicle with our own. Surprisingly, this often worked and we would spend the rest of the evening accompanying our new female friends around the fairground and, occasionally, escorting them back to their homes. The most entertaining of the static amusements, was the haunted house, not for its contents, which were not particularly scary, but for a small balcony on the upper storey of the building, visible to everyone in the fairground, over which all those in the house had to pass. From the floor of the balcony strong jets of air blew vertically upwards raising the loose skirts of the girls as they walked over it, Marilyn Monroe-style, to loud cheers from the male spectators below. Most of the unsuspecting victims rushed over the balcony holding down their skirts as best they could to preserve their modesty, a few walked slowly displaying stockings, suspenders and colourful underwear, delighting in their moment of infamy. My worst moment at the Pleasure Beach occurred when I attempted to impress a female companion with my prowess at hitting a punch ball. In trying to hit the ball as hard as I could, I overbalanced, totally missing the ball and succeeding only in landing my punch on the chin of a middle-aged woman standing nearby. Once I had ascertained that she was shaken but relatively unhurt, I quickly left the fairground in case of unpleasant repercussions. Naturally, my unimpressed female companion failed to leave with me.

In the 1950s Great Yarmouth, with its lively holiday season, provided much needed entertainment as well as employment for my family and me, and greatly compensated for our inability to take or even afford holidays away from home.

Endgame

'Fifty Years Ago', Benny Lee and the Stargazers, 1951

I hope that the previous pages have clearly illustrated that the 1950s were far from being a dull and colourless decade, but were a time when great changes took place – not only politically and economically, but also in the nature of leisure. Undoubtedly I found the times exciting because I was young and everything was new, but I cannot help thinking that life was full for most of my family and that entertaining and interesting opportunities existed to fill the leisure time of everybody, including a working class country boy like me. Nevertheless, as my recollections suggest, leisure-time activities did change during the decade mainly because of greater personal wealth, television and increasing car ownership.

In our home the greatest change occurred when my father bought our first television set. In the early 1950s, entertainment at home involved playing games, pursuing hobbies and developing handicraft skills, reading, writing and listening to the radio. By the end of the 1950s, watching television was the main leisure activity in the evenings and at weekends for most people, including my parents, especially when the advent of commercial television gave a greater choice of programmes. Television also affected entertainment outside the home as people became less inclined to venture out on cold winter evenings to visit the cinema, theatre and dance hall when an alternative entertainment existed inside their own comfortable living rooms. Gradually, my parents stopped attending whist drives and village dances, preferring instead to watch television at home, although they were tempted back to the village halls with the increasing popularity of bingo.

Government and local authority sponsorship in the late 1940s and early '50s encouraged a lively community spirit throughout the Flegg villages by providing the money to establish or modernise communal halls and recreation fields where, because of the limited availability of private and public transport to the leisure facilities of Great Yarmouth and Norwich, home-grown entertainments thrived. Hardly a night went by without a well-attended function or meeting taking place at a nearby village hall or playing field – whist, solo and beetle drives, cricket and football matches, film shows, dances and socials, drama, youth and women's clubs – all supported enthusiastically by the local village community. Growing car ownership throughout the decade had little initial effect on these activities, save for enabling more people to travel further for their entertainment. My parents regularly travelled in my father's car to distant Caister and even Great Yarmouth for whist drives and, eventually, bingo. I went to dances as far away as Hoveton, Wroxham and Horning on the back of a friend's motor scooter. In Great Yarmouth, car-owning jazz fans often provided lifts in their vehicles for other like-minded enthusiasts to jazz concerts in Norwich. I often travelled to jazz sessions with fans that I met in Diver's wine bar opposite the Regal on Regent Road. In sport, owning a car enabled some football and cricket players to join teams outside their home village, inevitably depriving many village teams of their best players and their village-only identities, and possibly contributing to the eventual decline and closure of many Flegg football and cricket clubs.

During the 1950s, the easy availability of employment, better pay and an improving economy not only provided a surplus of money in most people's pockets but also increased the quantity, quality and range of products it could buy. It is not surprising that the moment when I had money to spend, saved from pocket-money and casual employment, I found many things to spend it on – music, fashions and new forms of entertainment. Undoubtedly, as young people accumulated surplus income, it was inevitable that a youth-based culture would emerge that encouraged young people to spend money on fashions in clothing, popular music, Vespa and Lambretta scooters and acoustic guitars.

Throughout this book, I have described as accurately as I can the ways in which my family, friends and I filled our leisure time, and how that changed during the decade of the 1950s. I have tried not to be subjective in my comments, nor to suggest that life was more entertaining then, but simply to show the variety of activities that filled my leisure hours, how they changed through the decade and the significant differences between the 1950s and today.

Index